UNSTUCK

A GUIDE FOR LIVING IN UNCERTAIN TIMES

UNSTUCK

A GUIDE FOR LIVING IN UNCERTAIN TIMES

WITH LEADERS' GUIDE

AMERICAN BIBLE SOCIETY

Philadelphia

Unstuck: A Guide for Living in Uncertain Times

Contributors: Margi McCombs PhD, James Covey MA, Kalyn Lantz MA, Misty Bodkins MA, Eric Friesen, and Peter Edman MAR. *Thanks also to:* Philip Monroe PsyD, Brianna Leiendecker MA, Tameka Robinson, Laurie Fatica-Tice, Cindy Torres, and Victoria Raychynets.

UNSTUCK helps youth cope during times of uncertainty, especially after a disaster. The materials are written for young people to go through on their own and at their own pace. Participants will also benefit by working through the resource with experienced youth ministry workers in small groups over four or five weeks.

This resource is not intended to diagnose, treat, or cure any disease and does not take the place of professional counseling. Adult leaders should always partner with another adult when leading a group with youth and follow all local legal requirements.

This material is part of the **Beyond Disaster** suite. It can be used on its own or paired with related material for adults and children. See the website BeyondDisaster.Bible for more information and resources in several languages.

Expanded edition, January 2025. Some material is adapted with permission from *Life Hurts, Love Heals (Teen Journal)* and *Healing Teens' Wounds of Trauma: Facilitator Manual* by Margi McCombs, James Covey, and Kalyn Lantz. © 2017–2019 SIL International and American Bible Society.

Editor: Peter Edman
Illustrations: Ian Dale
Design: Shannon VanderWeide, Peter Edman

Unstuck (Participant PDF)	125642	978-1-58516-447-9
Unstuck (Participant Paperback/POD)	125641	978-1-58516-446-2
Unstuck (Leader PDF)	125758	978-1-58516-601-5
Unstuck (Leader Paperback/POD)	125759	978-1-58516-602-2

traumahealinginstitute.org

Resource provided by:

 **AMERICAN BIBLE SOCIETY**

101 North Independence Mall East FL8
Philadelphia PA 19106

What's Inside

Leaders' Guide

Welcome to *Unstuck: A Guide for Living in Uncertain Times.* This standalone program is designed for use with teens and youth during or after disruptions including natural disasters (earthquakes, tsunamis, hurricanes, floods, fires), epidemics, displacement, incidents of violence or abuse, or other stressful events. *Unstuck* was developed by the Trauma Healing Institute as a part of the **Beyond Disaster** suite of resources and draws from the Trauma Healing Institute teen curriculum.

This edition is focused on community violence, but it can also help youth learn to cope with other kinds of crises that can cause trauma, as well as ongoing issues like bullying. The storyline features a shooting, but readers in other tough circumstances will find that the characters react in ways that feel familiar. The questions, activities, and Bible spotlights apply to any stressful situation youth—or adults—will face.

If you are using *Unstuck* to respond to a disruptive event like a disaster, please note that the full program is most effective after some order has been reestablished. We recommend waiting for around six months. But even in the immediate aftermath of a trauma, the activities (especially those in Session 4) can prepare youth for physical and emotional reactions they will have.

Unstuck features five sessions. Four of the sessions begin with a story about a brother and sister who have just experienced a shooting at their high school, and the story in Session 4 looks at the same fictional incident from the perspective of another character. After each story, discussion questions, activities, and a Bible focus help participants identify and address their feelings and begin to recover hope in a broader context of God's ongoing care.

Unstuck can be used in several ways.

- As a journal for youth to work through at their own pace
- As a self-guided family exercise
- As a facilitated small-group session (four or five weeks, in person or online)
- As part of an after-school program

On the Trauma Healing Institute website, you can find adaptations of the program in other languages, along with the latest versions of this document and related resources for adults, youth, and children.

USING UNSTUCK WITH SMALL GROUPS

Training is not required to use this material, but leaders should read through this introduction carefully and prepare well. It is recommended that youth leaders participate in a healing group or attend an initial training for the Trauma Healing Institute's classic adult, teen, or children's curriculum before using this material.

Plan at least 90 minutes per session, plus a welcome or orientation session. Do not do all five sessions in one sitting. If you are pressed for time, Session 4 may be omitted. Session 4 can also be used as a standalone program.

Avoid lectures while leading sessions. Instead, focus on the material together. Your goal is not so much passing on information as it is asking helpful questions and guiding youth participants to a place where they can share their own stories and express their feelings.

Make plans with the youth participants to meet on a regular basis to discuss each chapter. They could either go through the materials as a group with the leader facilitating, or get together after they have completed each chapter on their own.

- When using the program in a group setting, there should be at least two adults at all times while facilitating the program.
- Choose facilitators/youth leaders who are already working with youth or teens, or who seem to fit the profile of a good youth leader (see below, page ix).
- As a team, review the sessions together before starting. Do the activities yourselves before you meet with the youth and be ready to share examples of what you have done.
- Learn and comply with the child safety policies and procedures of the ministry or church you are working with. Leaders must provide proof that they have met the legal requirements for the state or jurisdiction in which they live, which may include background checks and fingerprinting.
- Know the requirements for mandatory reporting laws that apply when you suspect physical or sexual abuse. Make sure that the youth know your legal reporting responsibilities and that they understand why you will need to comply. In the USA, Childwelfare.gov documents requirements for mandated reporting on child abuse.
- Contact parents/guardians of youth to tell them about the *Unstuck* material and ask permission to conduct a group using this material. Specify the location or online platform and the proposed timing.
- Provide informed-consent forms for the youth and parents/guardians (page 71).
- Develop and incorporate ground rules with the group before beginning Session 1 (see "Leading a Welcome Session" on page x).

PRACTICAL TIPS FOR GROUPS

- Each participant should have their own *Unstuck* **booklet** or digital download. Emphasize that their responses in the books are personal and private, and will only be shared if they choose.
- Make sure all participants have access to a **Bible,** either printed or online, at an appropriate reading level. The *Contemporary English Version, Good News Translation, New Living Translation,* and *English Standard Version* are all used in these materials.
- If this will be an online group, make sure all participants have the appropriate **app** installed on their computers or phones. Include the group link in each message. Avoid using presentation software so people can see each other's faces.
- Consider creating a private group or **message board** online. *Have a plan to monitor any forum you create.* You could use this forum to encourage participants while going through the *Unstuck* material with reminder texts ("Are you feeling stuck in UNSTUCK?) and teasers ("Have you done the volcano thing yet?").
- Participants might want to share their **responses** to several activities in the booklet. Suggest that they take a picture of their finished drawings, videos, or written content and post it during meetings or on your private group or message board.
- If your group is large, break into **small groups** of two to four people for discussion. If online, use the breakout room feature on your meeting app. Have an experienced adult facilitator participate in each online breakout room. You may want to debrief in the large group after each small group.
- Consider beginning each session with a brief **icebreaker** activity. **Recap** highlights of your previous times together, as well as the group's ground rules, before starting a new session.

- The **Box Breathing** exercise is introduced in Session 2. Remember that this deep breathing activity can be helpful across the rest of the sessions and also something participants can continue to do on their own.

GETTING UP TO SPEED

In this guide, you will find background and tips for the activities in *Unstuck,* showing how they can help people begin to heal from traumatic experiences.

If you are not a current trauma healing facilitator, it is important for you to review this guide and do the activities for yourself. One reason is to help you identify and begin to process any past painful or traumatic experiences of your own so you are prepared for emotions that might arise in yourself during group discussions. You need a basic understanding of the effects of trauma, how to recognize our feelings, the effects of being heard, and how to express our grief in lament.

If you are new to the *Healing the Wounds of Trauma* model, you can also visit traumahealingbasics. org and explore the helpful tools there. Brief videos and digital downloads will help you learn to identify trauma and recognize its impact. You can start with What is Trauma (video), Healing from Trauma (video), Recognizing Trauma (PDF document), and The Journey of Healing (video).

WORKING WITH TRAUMATIZED YOUTH

While *Unstuck* is written to be self-explanatory and does not require leader certification, we do encourage its use by people who already have some experience working with youth. Working with youth who have experienced trauma can be challenging since their emotional wounds can show up in difficult behavior. It takes an experienced youth worker to be able to respond lovingly, appropriately, and with wise behavior management and safe engagement. Here are some things to remember.

- Trauma of any kind leaves emotional wounds that must be addressed for healthy ongoing development.
- If these heart wounds are not addressed, there will be long-term negative effects on physical health, social behavior, and ability to maintain long-term relationships.
- There is no trauma that cannot be healed. It may take a long time, but God is able to heal shattered hearts.

HOW DOES TRAUMA AFFECT YOUTH?

Trauma affects the whole person, but it can be helpful to distinguish various aspects.

1. **Emotional effects**

   - They may become angry and aggressive. Younger teens may fight with their peers more than before and may challenge their parents, caregivers, and teachers more.
   - They may become sad and depressed, isolating themselves and losing interest in life.
   - They may suffer extreme mood swings.
   - They may feel responsible for what happened and suffer feelings of guilt and shame.
   - They may feel "survivor guilt" because they survived the trauma and others did not.
   - They may show a lack of empathy for others.

2. **Physical effects**

- Their speech may be affected. They may begin to stutter or become mute.
- They may exhibit eating disorders, where they lose their appetite because they are anxious, or they eat too much to try to lessen the pain.
- They may complain of headaches, stomachaches, or other aches and pains in their bodies.
- They may have an increased autoimmune response such as hives or asthma.

3. **Behavioral effects**

- They may have sleep disorders—nightmares or screaming in their sleep without being awake. They may have trouble getting to sleep.
- They may stir up conflicts or initiate domestic violence, bullying, and so on.
- They may cry easily and often.
- They may have difficulty focusing and learning new things.
- They may use alcohol or drugs to lessen their pain.
- They may disengage through the use of social media or gaming.
- They may become involved in sexual promiscuity.
- They may engage in risky behavior to help them feel brave in the face of danger.
- They may hurt themselves by cutting their bodies or attempting or committing suicide.
- They may choose friends or groups that are risky to their well-being but make them feel safe.

HOW CAN WE HELP TRAUMATIZED YOUTH?

There are many ways we can help. Here are some ideas. We can:

- Provide a safe place where trust can be restored.
- Invite youth into a loving, judgment-free relationship.
- Listen to their stories.
- Assure that their basic needs are met.
- Let them know they are not alone.
- Introduce them to the Bible's wisdom and the loving, comforting, faithful presence of Jesus.
- Encourage trauma-informed families, churches, and communities.
- Give them a voice in their families and communities.
- Establish long-term relationships with them.
- Help them find ways to contribute to the well-being of others.
- Provide structure and routines.

Ideally, work through one session at a time and take breaks as necessary to ensure they are not feeling overwhelmed.

CREATING THE RIGHT ENVIRONMENT

Youth (like children and adults) want to be loved, supported, and encouraged. Their life experiences often teach them that expressing this need shows weakness—and weakness is a liability, especially for traumatized teens. Often teens and youth have the same needs as a child but have started to learn adult coping strategies. Emotional walls of protection have been built and are not easy to cross.

Far more important than the group being fun or "cool" is that the experience is welcoming, nonjudgmental, inclusive, and emotionally safe. The best healing environment for youth (and for most people) is a place where participants feel safe enough to be themselves and confident they can share their thoughts and stories without fear of ridicule.

This can be challenging because a common defense mechanism for emotionally wounded youth is to laugh or put others down. This reaction protects their insecurity but will lead to hostility and insecurity in other group members. At your first gathering, guide the group in making ground rules that will encourage everyone to participate fully (see "Leading a Welcome Session" on page x).

While we want to foster a good environment for sharing, youth leaders may also have other responsibilities. It may be part of your role to gently correct. Leaders can help youth recognize that they have choices, and that these choices affect the direction of their lives. If participants in your group need guidance, a discussion of **PSALM 1** (comparing the fruitful tree and the wind-blown chaff) may help them make that connection. See Option 2 for the closing of the Welcome session, below.

Learning to Be a Good Listener

Listening is the most basic way leaders can help youth process secondary trauma or a crisis moment. The Trauma Healing Institute has developed a set of three simple but effective questions you can ask to create space for a person to share a painful experience.

LISTENING QUESTION	WHY IT HELPS
1. What happened?	It orients the listener and can lead into deeper discussion. It helps the person sort out facts and timeline.
2. How did you feel?	Since healing takes place at the level of emotions, it helps to name them. Being heard with compassion can start the healing process.
3. What was the hardest part for you?	It can help both the person sharing and the listener to better understand the effects of what happened. It keeps the listener from thinking they already know the answer.

Profile of a Good Youth Leader

Effective leaders must:

- Be genuinely interested in the youth they are working with
- Be ready to listen and learn
- Be emotionally stable themselves
- Be committed to the healing of the heart—the emotions and spirit
- Know their own limitations
- Be grounded in their faith
- Love people in this age group

Effective youth leaders aren't afraid to laugh at themselves. They get involved in activities with the kids, and they know how to keep that delicate balance of having fun and relating to youth without trying to become their peers.

Referrals

Trauma Healing Institute materials are not attempting to provide mental health care or to replace the need for mental health professionals such as a counselor or psychologist. Leaders should be prepared for situations that require professional help for the youth in their care, and should have established relationships with qualified mental health professionals for referrals before launching into using *Unstuck* with youth.

LEADING A WELCOME SESSION

Groups using *Unstuck* should start with an opening session to orient the group and set expectations. Make this longer or shorter to fit your group, but the session should include:

- A high-level overview of the sessions
- Introductions
- A discussion of ground rules and confidentiality
- A brief Bible passage

OVERVIEW

Introduce yourself and the other leaders as necessary. Give a brief recap of the Welcome text (page 1) and summarize some of the learning objectives in the "Overview of the Sessions" below. Emphasize that *Unstuck* is designed to be interactive but that their reflections in the journal are private unless they choose to share.

INTRODUCTIONS

If the youth do not know each other, go around and share names and a favorite food or activity.

If time permits, try a low-pressure icebreaker activity like "This or That." The leader gives two choices and each participant must decide which one they choose (in person, have participants move to two designated sides of the room; online, have participants raise a hand or signal their choice). The leader should do two rounds (example: beaches or mountains) and then let each participant take a turn coming up with the choices. Choice categories could include sports, music, pop culture, food, social media apps, and the like.

GROUND RULES AND CONFIDENTIALITY

Ask the group to help create a brief list of "group agreements." Make sure all the youth get a chance to contribute their ideas. Such guidelines can help prevent bullying and make space for everyone to participate. Good guidelines include:

- attending every session,
- showing respect to one another,
- making sure everyone gets a chance to speak, and
- not allowing put-downs.

If confidentiality is not mentioned, prompt a discussion about the importance of committing to each other to keep what is shared in the group private. Remind the group of the mandatory reporting rules in the informed consent document.

CLOSING

If participants are not familiar with the Bible, you may need to introduce it briefly (here or at another point) and show how to navigate a print or digital Bible. The Bible offers time-tested wisdom for people of every culture, and it introduces us to a God who loves us and guides us through life.

Option 1: End your welcome session with a reading of **PSALM 23.** Mention that God knows and cares about what each of the participants are going through.

Option 2: Read **PSALM 1 (NLT** or **CEV).** Depending on time available, you can invite the participants to talk together about some of these questions.

UNSTUCK: A Guide for Living in Uncertain Times

- This psalm is about choices. What two kinds of people does it talk about? Where do their paths lead?
- Look at verse 1. Whose advice shapes your view of the world (thinking)? Whose example do you imitate (behavior)? What groups and friendships shape your identity (belonging)?
- Look at verse 2. What does the psalm say about where we should find happiness? (The word "Law" is also translated "instruction," "teaching," and "direction.")
- Look at verses 3 and 4. Are you feeling more aimless and dry, or rooted and fruitful?

Then say something like, "We can't avoid life's storms. How does the psalm help you think about staying grounded (but not stuck)? Over the next five sessions, we will look at ways to respond well no matter what happens around us."

OVERVIEW OF THE SESSIONS

By the end of each session, participants should understand several concepts and have begun to explore tools to help them apply the concepts to their own lives.

Leaders should help the participants draw connections between the stories and the activities. For instance, in Session 4, Daniel's response to the balloon popping is an example of a trigger. We see his stress response. We also see how talking with Coach Jay helped him begin to calm down.

Session 0. Welcome
- The stories and activities in *Unstuck* can help me get through hard times.
- I know the ground rules for the group.
- I know this group is a confidential space.
- I am starting to know the other participants.
- The Bible teaches that God knows and cares about what I'm going through.

Session 1: Why am I feeling this way?
- We all have complex feelings.
- Our feelings come to the surface in our behaviors.
- I can name some of the losses I have experienced and some of my feelings about them.
- In the Bible, Elijah experienced a range of feelings and brought them to God.

Session 2: What can I do with these feelings?
- We can recognize ways we are responding to our situations.
- We can recognize feelings and how they impact our bodies.
- I know practical ways to care for myself.
- I know how to manage strong feelings with a breathing exercise.
- I can express my honest feelings to God.
- In the Bible, David shows several different healthy ways of responding to stress and loss.

Session 3: How can I get unstuck?
- Sharing your story with someone you feel safe with is a good way to begin healing.
- Three important questions can help people tell their stories.
- It is important to be heard, and to know who I can talk to.
- I know some things I have control over, even when things are out of control.
- There are many ways to tell my story.
- In the Bible, Job's friends did not listen well to him. God is powerful and is happy to listen to our questions.

TIPS AND TIMETABLE

Here is a suggested timetable for leading a group through *Unstuck.* Adapt this to your needs and the time available. Several of the activities work well as homework.

- **Recommended timetable.** Pilot tests for this program suggest giving 90 minutes for each full session, plus time for the Welcome session. This gives the youth enough time to talk.
- **Shorter timetable.** Groups can also be effective in 60 minutes per session if leaders assign some of the activities in each session as homework. Online check-ins or reminders can help maintain momentum and connection between gatherings.
- **Multi-week timetable.** If you are meeting with youth for 30 minutes at a time, each of the sessions can be broken into three parts: (1) the story and first activity at the first meeting, (2) the next few activities as a second meeting (or homework), and (3) the concluding session featuring the last activity and the Bible spotlight.

Begin each session with an icebreaker activity, a recap of ground rules (if needed), and a recap of prior topics. Get feedback from any homework.

	TIPS	TIME
Session 0. Welcome (see page x)		**30 min**
Introductions	Use an icebreaker if you have time.	10 min
Overview	Don't cover all the objectives, just enough to orient them on the overall structure	5 min
Ground Rules & Confidentiality		10 min
Closing	Be sure to select a strong reader, or read the Bible passage out loud yourself.	5 min

	TIPS	TIME
Session 1. Why Am I Feeling This Way?		**90 min**
Story: Goodbye, Normal	One of the leaders should read the stories.	20–30 min
Activity: Name Your Feelings		10–15 min
Activity: Name Your Losses	This activity can be assigned as homework.	15 min
Activity: Anger Volcano	See if the group is comfortable sharing some of the things they wrote. Learning how other people react may help them talk more freely.	10 min
Bible Spotlight: Elijah Runs		20 min
Session 2. What Can I Do With These Feelings?		**90 min**
Story: Roll Credits, Please		20–30 min
Activity: Body Scan	In a group, draw the body outline on a board or flip chart. Focus on one feeling, like anger. Have participants give examples of where they feel anger in their body. Cover other feelings if time permits.	15 min
Activity: Taking Care of Yourself	This activity can be assigned as homework.	15 min
Activity: Box Breathing	Do the box breathing together three to five times as a group, then read the verse slowly, if appropriate. Give an opportunity for feedback and suggest that participants try doing this routinely (like at bedtime).	5 min
Bible Spotlight: David's Feelings		20 min
Session 3. How Can I Get Unstuck?		**90 min**
Story: Connecting Through the Crazy		20 min
Activity: Telling Your Story	It may help to discuss why the questions help us listen well (page ix). After participants have had a chance to write out their story using the bullseye image, give them time to share with one another. If time is short, assign this as homework. Ask them to find someone this week to practice sharing their story with. *Optional:* As part of this assignment, or separately, have them practice listening to others. To prepare them, say or write: "Tell someone you know about the Telling Your Story activity. Have the person think of something small but painful that happened to them. Then use the three questions to help them tell their story." At your next gathering, ask how it felt to share (or to listen).	20 min

	TIPS	TIME
Activity: Circle of Control	This can be done as a large-group activity with the circle of control on a flip chart. Participants can record personal notes in their journals.	10 min
Activity: Map Your Goals	This activity can be assigned as homework.	15 min
Activity: The Next Good Thing	This activity can be assigned as homework. In group, consider asking for other ideas that participants can do as a group or with friends.	5 min
Bible Spotlight: Listening with Job		20 min
Session 4. What Is Happening Inside of Me?		**90 min**
Story: Life on a Hair Trigger		20–30 min
Activity: Hiding Our Feelings	*Supplies:* You need plastic water bottles and a bucket of water for this activity. *Option 1:* Use ping pong balls instead of bottles. *Option 2:* Write the feelings on small blown-up balloons, which you can later pop to release the air. Videos of this activity are linked on page 62.	15 min
Activity: How Our Brains React to Danger	An optional video resource for this activity is linked on page 62.	15 min
Activity: Triggers		10 min
Activity: Color Your Pain	This activity can be assigned as homework.	10 min
Bible Spotlight: A Range of Feelings	Select a few of the verses, or divide them among small groups.	20 min
Session 5. How Can I Relate to God in Uncertain Times?		**90 min**
Story: Elevate the Complaint		20–30 min
Activity: Grief Street	If you do this with a group, you can draw the journey and have the group share some ways you would feel or have felt at those stops.	20 min
Activity: Creating a Lament	This activity can be assigned as homework.	15 min
Activity: My Manifesto	Encourage youth to be creative and add colors. If it would be helpful, add time for participants who want to share parts of their manifesto with the group. This activity can be assigned as homework.	10 min
Bible Spotlight: Peace, Be Still		15 min

Welcome

UNSTUCK: A GUIDE FOR LIVING IN UNCERTAIN TIMES

When disasters or tragedies happen, our lives are interrupted and we suddenly face uncertain times. You might be feeling alone right now, missing friends and opportunities, dealing with difficult circumstances, and finding it hard to stay motivated to do anything at all. You may have lost material belongings or even a loved one who has died in the midst of these hard days.

Maybe you're feeling stuck right now, and don't know how to get yourself going again. It's hard to know how to move forward when you don't know how long things will be like this, or if life will ever feel normal again.

The activities in this book can be helpful in getting you through this crisis—or any time your life gets turned upside down. There are five sessions for you to experience, but don't try to do them all at once! Space them out in a way that seems right for you.

Each session begins with a story. In the main, four-part story, Rosa and Phoenix are living through the aftermath of a shooting at their school. In the story for Session 4, Daniel experiences the same event from his own perspective.

Your circumstances will be different from theirs, but you may see that their responses are similar to your own. We hope you'll find comfort from God's presence and some guidance and strategies for getting UNSTUCK as you go through these sessions.

UNSTUCK is designed to be used either in a group setting (with a family or small group), or by yourself (in self-guided journaling). If you're using UNSTUCK as a journal, it can be helpful to share some of the activities with someone you trust.

Why Am I Feeling This Way?

GOODBYE, NORMAL

It seemed like shootings were on the news every day. But they were always happening somewhere else, affecting other people. It wasn't that Rosa didn't care —it was just that when you kept hearing the same sad story on loop, even terrible events could fade into the background, and you grew . . . numb.

But suddenly it wasn't in the background—it was terrifyingly up in her business. Someone pulled a gun at one of her basketball games. Now, a week later, Rosa and her younger brother Phoenix were trying to live their lives in a world that felt less predictable.

Rosa had been loving her senior year of high school. As a star player on the girls' team, she was constantly surrounded by friends. She also worked part time at the local coffee shop and was saving some money.

Life wasn't so great for Phoenix. He was a freshman in a new school while his longtime circle of friends got to stay together in another school. He was lonely and felt embarrassed that everything was so hard. His grades had taken a hit, and he couldn't connect with anyone—definitely not his parents. They both worked and were always fighting, usually about money. Mostly it was just yelling. Phoenix couldn't find the energy to talk to either of them about his struggles. They would probably just start yelling at him too, so he just avoided everything. No matter which way he turned, there was more and more stress.

The shooting made everything worse. Rosa was on the court when it happened. She was so caught up in the game that she hadn't even noticed the scuffle in the stands. Some said it started when a parent got upset over a referee's call. Others thought someone threw something at the fans from the other team. Rosa never got it straight. There were a bunch of different stories on social media. All she knew was that parents were involved, and then suddenly everyone was involved.

Rosa had been waving her arms, trying to get Laura to pass her the ball, when a deafening gunshot boomed across the gym. Rosa felt a buzz and heard Natalie cry out. She realized her friend was lying on the floor, holding her leg.

They caught the guy with the gun. Natalie went to the hospital and got her leg bandaged up. The bullet had only grazed her. Luckily, no one else was hurt. Since the shooting happened after school hours, the district canceled extracurricular activities for the rest of the year, let everyone stay home from school for a couple days, and called it good.

But it wasn't good for Rosa. Not even close. "That's it?" She slammed her book down on her bedroom desk. "They're going to just cancel the best season our team has ever had?"

Still, part of her was relieved that she wouldn't have to go back out on the basketball court. She didn't think she could handle it. The first day back to school had been bad enough. The crowded hallways. The noise. Every little unexpected sound made her jump and sent her heart pounding in horror. In her mind, it felt like she was watching Natalie bleed out on the court on repeat. She spent much of that first day back hiding in the girls' bathroom, trying to catch her breath and fighting a sick stomach. "What's wrong with me?" she wondered.

Rosa's parents didn't argue when she said she wasn't going back to school. In fact, they encouraged it. "I don't want you going back there," her mom told her. "I've spoken to a lot of parents, and you're not the only one staying home. It's not safe."

Money was tight, so their parents couldn't stay home with Rosa. For his own safety and the sake of his sister, they insisted Phoenix stay home too. He wasn't thrilled by the news. "This is just going to make everything harder," he said. He flipped through his social media feeds, reading everybody's take on the shooting. And all the posts about a recent trip his old friends had taken together—it looked like the most amazing experience ever. "At least someone is having a good time," he muttered.

Phoenix sighed, his head crowded with thoughts. "Like school isn't hard enough. How am I going to keep up my grades from home—especially with our ancient computer? Is Rosa going to be okay? How am I supposed to make friends if I'm stuck here? What if there's another shooting?" Phoenix suddenly felt very tired, and so overwhelmed that he fell asleep on the couch with an ache in his chest and tears in his eyes.

In her bedroom, Rosa put in her earbuds and hugged her pillow tighter. Like Phoenix, her mind was racing. "Am I always going to feel like this? What about all my plans? It's

	UNSTUCK: A Guide for Living in Uncertain Times

my last year of school! I feel completely stuck. My whole life is just on hold. Will I ever feel safe—or normal—again? What if I had been nearer when they pulled the trigger? It's like my life's smashed into a brick wall. What even comes next?"

Rosa buried her head into her pillow and cried. 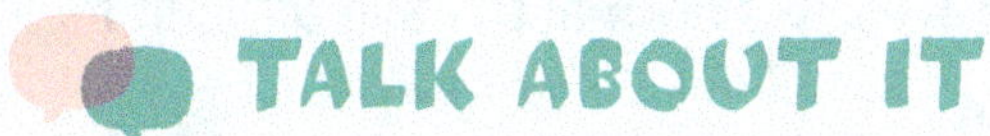

TALK ABOUT IT

Put your thoughts into words or draw a picture to answer the following questions. If you're with a group, talk about these together.

1. What happened to Phoenix and Rosa? What are some of the ways they are feeling?

2. What are some of the things Rosa has lost? What are some of the things Phoenix has lost? Why does Rosa feel "stuck"?

3. What are some ways you can relate to Rosa and Phoenix's situation? When have you experienced similar feelings?

NAME YOUR FEELINGS

It's good to notice your feelings, especially during days when many things have changed for you. There are no "wrong" feelings! Feelings are a natural response to things that happen in our lives. It is normal to have difficult feelings when difficult things happen to us.

Circle any words below that describe the feelings you've experienced recently.

ANGRY   DISAPPOINTED   SAD   EXCITED   FRUSTRATED

RELAXED   ANXIOUS   WORRIED   HOPELESS   ASHAMED

GUILTY   CALM   DEPRESSED   JEALOUS   LONELY

HOPEFUL   BORED   HAPPY   NUMB   CONFUSED

OVERWHELMED   HELPLESS   AFRAID   REJECTED

TALK ABOUT IT

1. Why is it sometimes difficult to talk about your feelings?

2. Which of these feelings are the strongest for you right now?

3. Do you have other feelings you can name?

4. What do you do when you feel this way?

NAME YOUR LOSSES

How has a current or recent situation interrupted your life? Think about opportunities you may have lost, the disappointment of canceled events, the interruption of your plans, not knowing when this "life-on-hold" feeling is going to end or what the "new normal" will be. Perhaps relationships with some important people in your life have changed and you've lost a feeling of connection with them.

See if you can name the losses you have experienced as a result of your situation. Remember they may be physical things like friends, school, and sports, or deeper things like personal freedom or safety. Then, write how each loss makes you feel, or draw a face showing that feeling.

WHAT I HAVE LOST	HOW IT MAKES ME FEEL

ANGER VOLCANO

You might be feeling more anger than usual these days. For many people, anger is the most difficult emotion to understand and to control. Did you know that anger doesn't exist on its own? Anger usually comes from another underlying emotion we are feeling, and most of the time we don't even realize it. We use anger to protect ourselves or to cover up other feelings that make us feel vulnerable.

This picture of a volcano can help us understand our anger. Look back to the earlier activities and check out the feelings you circled and named. Some of those feelings may have erupted into anger, even though you didn't notice what you were feeling at the time. You just knew you were angry.

In the illustration of the volcano, write in the section underground the feelings that you have that sometimes erupt into anger. In the air above the volcano where the anger erupts, write some of the things you have done when you're angry.

Feeling anger is not bad. It tells us that something is wrong, that we are feeling something we need to deal with in healthy ways.

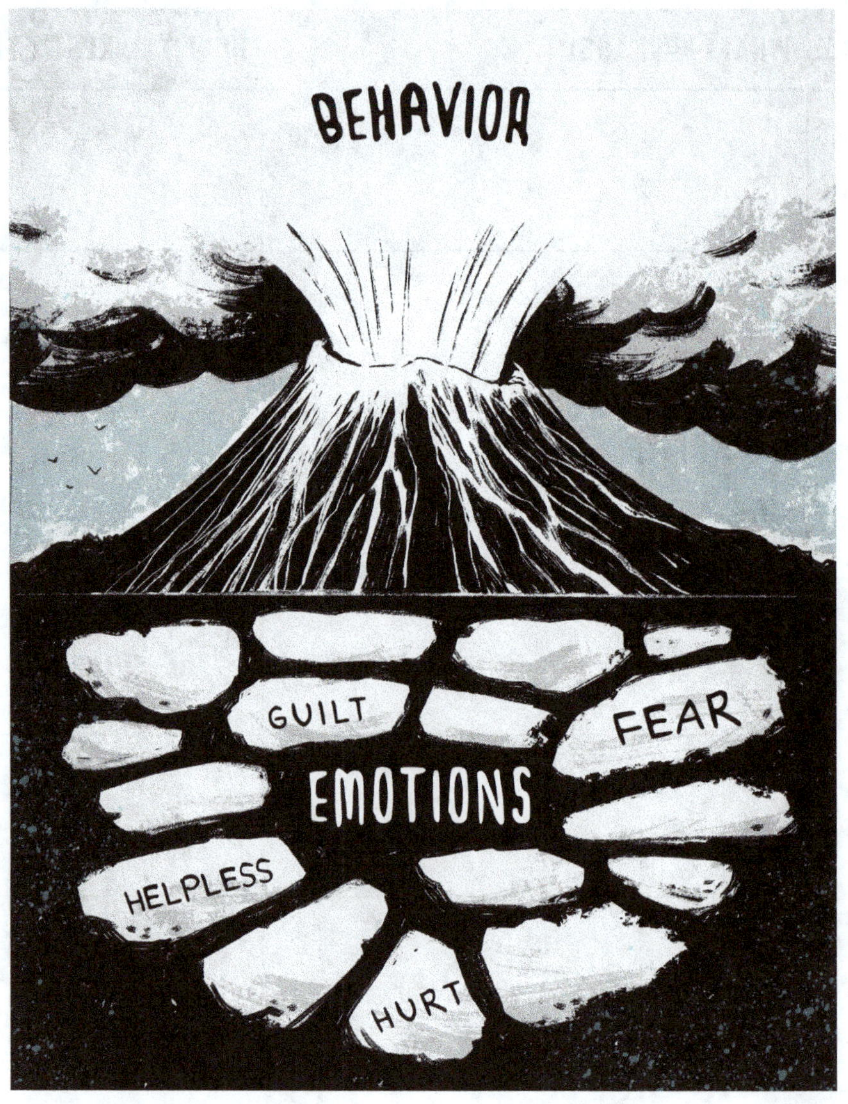

ELIJAH RUNS

Elijah is one of the Bible's greatest and best-known prophets—someone authorized to speak and act for God. He lived around 860 BC, when King Ahab of Israel abandoned God and Ahab's wife Jezebel led God's people to worship Baal, the local fertility god.

God told Elijah to confront the king, and he began by declaring a drought that lasted three years. During the drought, God provided miraculously for Elijah (**1 KINGS 17**). And God ended the drought on Elijah's request—after a famous (and funny) confrontation between Elijah and 450 prophets of Baal. King Ahab watched as God revealed himself with fire from heaven and the people helped Elijah kill the false prophets (**1 KINGS 18**).

Imagine how Elijah is feeling. God speaks to him, provides for him. He has stood up to the king and faced thousands of people—and been vindicated. Everything is going his way. It's an emotional high! You might imagine that nothing could shake his faith and his confidence in God's protection. But then Ahab goes home, and the next chapter begins:

> Ahab told his wife Jezebel what Elijah had done and that he had killed the prophets. She sent a message to Elijah: "You killed my prophets. Now I'm going to kill you! I pray that the gods will punish me even more severely if I don't do it by this time tomorrow."
>
> Elijah was afraid when he got her message, and he ran to the town of Beersheba in Judah. He left his servant there, then walked another whole day into the desert. Finally, he came to a large bush and sat down in its shade. He begged the LORD, "I've had enough. Just let me die! I'm no better off than my ancestors." Then he lay down in the shade and fell asleep.
>
> Suddenly an angel woke him up and said, "Get up and eat." Elijah looked around, and by his head was a jar of water and some baked bread. He sat up, ate and drank, then lay down and went back to sleep.
>
> Soon the LORD's angel woke him again and said, "Get up and eat, or else you'll get too tired to travel." So Elijah sat up and ate and drank.
>
> The food and water made him strong enough to walk forty more days. At last, he reached Mount Sinai, the mountain of God, and he spent the night there in a cave.

While Elijah was on Mount Sinai, the LORD asked, "Elijah, why are you here?"

He answered, "LORD God All-Powerful, I've always done my best to obey you. But your people have broken their solemn promise to you. They have torn down your altars and killed all your prophets, except me. And now they are even trying to kill me!"

"Go out and stand on the mountain," the LORD replied. "I want you to see me when I pass by."

All at once, a strong wind shook the mountain and shattered the rocks. But the LORD was not in the wind. Next, there was an earthquake, but the LORD was not in the earthquake. Then there was a fire, but the LORD was not in the fire.

Finally, there was a soft whisper, and when Elijah heard it, he covered his face with his coat. He went out and stood at the entrance to the cave.

The LORD asked, "Elijah, why are you here?"

Elijah answered, "LORD God All-Powerful, I've always done my best to obey you. But your people have broken their solemn promise to you. They have torn down your altars and killed all your prophets, except me. And now they are even trying to kill me!"

1 KINGS 19:1–14 CEV

Twice God asks the same question, and gets the exact same answer. Elijah sounds stuck!

But each time, God responds with more perspective. Now he tells Elijah that changes are about to happen. Justice is coming, and the prophet is given a new task.

God tells Elijah who to appoint as new kings for Israel and Syria—and who to appoint as his own assistant and successor as prophet. God also tells him that 7,000 other people in Israel are standing with him. He is not alone. And Elijah does what God commanded (**1 KINGS 19:15–21**).

1. What has Elijah lost? What feelings can you recognize in this story? Circle words or phrases that identify them. What did Elijah do in response to his feelings?

2. How does God respond to Elijah and his complaints? Is this what you would have expected of God?

3. Why does God want Elijah to stand on the mountain? What do you think God is showing Elijah? Why does God ask the same question twice?

4. Have you experienced feelings that are similar to those Elijah felt? What did you do in response to those feelings?

5. When you are struggling, do you find it more encouraging to remember God's power (shattering mountains and naming kings), or God's "soft whisper" and patient questions?

God was present and patient with the struggles and weakness of a great leader. He continues to be present and patient with us, too. In your Bible, find the book of Psalms and look for **PSALM 34**. In verse 18, it says, "The LORD is near to the brokenhearted and saves the crushed in spirit."

Just as God was with Elijah and invited him to share his experiences, know that God is with you now in your pain and grief.

Take a Break!

Thinking and journaling about difficult emotions can be tiring.
If you're going through *Unstuck* on your own,
be sure to take breaks between chapters.

What Can I Do With These Feelings?

ROLL CREDITS, PLEASE

T*his is just like a movie—a horror movie,* Rosa thought. *Trapped at home. Waiting for somebody to jump out at you. Nobody makes it to the end in those kinds of movies, do they? Will I?*

It was hard not to focus on the growing list of misfortune. First the basketball season got canceled and then most extracurricular activities . . . during her senior year. No championships, no parties, no prom. Even worse, as her days at home turned into weeks, her grades began to weigh on her. She could barely muster the strength to see what homework was due. Before the shooting, she'd been hoping to do well and get into a better college. Now with the season canceled, she wondered if she could even count on an athletic scholarship.

She had never thought it was possible to have so many things taken away at once. She felt like she was slowly suffocating beneath a stack of heavy blankets and someone kept piling more on. She didn't have the energy to keep in shape—couldn't even stand the thought of going out for a run. Her boss at the coffee shop kept calling, but she just ignored the phone.

Her friends tried to help. For a while, her teammate Laura would drop by after school. One day, sitting on Rosa's bedroom floor, Laura started digging through her bag. "You're too uptight, Rosa. You need something to help you relax and forget what happened." She handed over a joint.

Rosa hesitated. She'd never smoked anything before. *Laura never lets it get out of control,* she thought. The promise of forgetting was too tempting. She extended the joint toward Laura's lighter. In the end, though, there wasn't much forgetting—just a lot of coughing.

Phoenix was struggling too. He hated being stuck at home. He and Rosa had never spent much time together, but now she mostly kept to her room, and they barely saw each other.

Every once in a while he would go out for a walk, and that helped clear his head a little. Then dad discovered he hadn't been staying at home. Their dad had been at Rosa's game and was one of the first parents to run onto the court after Natalie was shot. Even though Rosa hadn't been physically hurt, he'd become increasingly worried and constantly called from work to check up on them. Phoenix didn't want to answer the call while he was out walking, but it would have been worse if he hadn't.

"Why do I hear cars in the background?" his dad demanded. "Are you outside? What are you thinking—you trying to get shot?"

"No!" Phoenix shouted back. "That doesn't even make any sense. Our neighborhood isn't dangerous or anything!"

"Tell that to your sister," his dad muttered. "Stay in the house—I don't want you wandering."

Phoenix was cooped up with the silent ghost of his sister. His mom was also away most of the time—or sleeping. She worked long shifts at the clinic. Phoenix was half convinced she'd signed onto their dad's overprotective mentality because she felt guilty over being at work during the shooting.

Phoenix spent a lot of time messaging his old friends, but he still felt out of touch. They offered some support, but they were doing their own things without him now and their responses were getting slower and less frequent. When they did bother to reply, it seemed disconnected . . . fake. He would scream if he got one more sad emoji.

He obsessed over the social feeds on the shooting. He hadn't been at the game himself. He hated sports and wouldn't step foot in a gym even to cheer on Rosa's team. But he thought that maybe if he could figure out what happened that night, he'd feel better— more in control. It didn't turn out that way, though. Everyone had a different angle on the shooting and some of them were weird.

One day Rosa made a rare appearance and wandered into the kitchen. She caught Phoenix staring blankly at his homework. "Hey, what are you doing?"

It took a moment for him to register what she said, and then everything inside boiled over. "What's it look like?" he slammed down his book. "Nothing!" He stormed off to his bedroom.

Phoenix felt bad for doing so poorly at his new school. He knew how important school was to his future, but he was lonely. Plus, he preferred drawing and gaming to math and science, and now he was so far behind it hardly felt worth trying to catch up. His teacher was trying to talk to his parents, but Phoenix kept deleting the emails and intercepting the phone calls.

When he felt bad, he'd lay in his bed and stare at the ceiling for what felt like hours. He felt so trapped: stuck at home, behind in school, no friends. Now he focused on a crack overhead until his vision grew watery and the tears ran onto his pillow.

💬 TALK ABOUT IT

1. Why did life seem like a horror movie to Rosa and Phoenix?

2. What was each member of the family feeling during this situation, and how were they each responding to those feelings?

3. What are some ways that you have been responding to your situation? Do you think of your responses as positive or negative?

BODY SCAN

Have you ever had a headache before a test or felt your stomach tossing around because of a conflict with someone? That's because our physical bodies hold our stress and emotions.

Have you ever been grouchy when you missed lunch? That's because it can work the other way too. Good or bad health in our body can also touch our mind and our spirit.

Our bodies communicate how we are feeling, often even before we are aware of how stressful times are affecting us. Consider all the different and difficult things going on in your life right now. Thinking about all of that at once can be really hard!

TRY IT! Take a minute to scan your body. Do this by focusing on each different part of your body and noticing what you feel physically. It could be pain, tightness, discomfort, tingling, or any other kind of sensation. Start at your head and slowly go down your neck, shoulders, arms, chest, stomach, back, waist, legs, and feet. Pause at each area and focus on what you feel.

On the body outline shown here, mark the location where you noticed a feeling in your own body. After you think about each area, do your best to relax the muscles there and let go of the stress you're feeling. Then move on.

Finish up by taking a few minutes to write down what you felt and where you felt it.

You can do a body scan anytime, day or night, to help relax your body—it also helps relax your mind—and lower your stress levels. Paying attention to what your body is feeling helps you know when you are stressed and need to do something to take care of yourself.

TAKING CARE OF YOURSELF

Three ways to take care of your body:

1. **Move.** It is super important to move your body. Moving around increases oxygen to your cells for extra energy and helps you feel better by releasing the hormones called endorphins.

   - If you are able to be outdoors, make time to do that every day. Sunlight positively affects mood, and physical activity can improve concentration and a sense of well-being.
   - If you are stuck indoors, try bodyweight exercises, movements you can do using your body's weight for resistance (like pushups, squats, and lunges). Dancing along with your favorite videos also count! If you can get online, there are endless free resources and apps to guide you in exercising in your home.

   TRY IT! Take five minutes now to stop and go outside for a walk—or dance, stretch, or do something else that's active!

2. **Eat healthy.** Keeping your body healthy is especially important in stressful times. It also helps keep your spirits up when you are under stress. Snack food and junk food are designed to be easy to eat. But they aren't the best things for you, especially if you sit a lot. Try to drink only water for a day. Eat foods that nourish and are more filling whenever you can. Cooking for yourself and your family can also be a good way to help out, eat better, and feel better.

3. **Limit screen time.** It seems like everyone is saying it, but take some time away from screens (phone, computer, television), especially before bedtime. Try setting a timer for thirty minutes or an hour to remind yourself to take a ten-minute break (or longer) to do other things that take care of your body, mind, or spirit.

Three ways to take care of your mind:

1. **Avoid panic.** Keeping your thoughts under control has a positive effect on other dimensions of life. When you feel anxious, take the time to write out what your anxious thoughts are. It is a way to take our thoughts "captive," as **2 CORINTHIANS 10:5** notes. Remind yourself: Right now, I'm safe. Stay in the present.

2. **Choose your focus.** Think about what you are thinking about. That may sound crazy, but if you spend all day thinking about stressful things, guess what? You're going to feel stressed. Instead, choose good things to focus your attention on. Set time limits on reading news and social feeds. Use healthy distractions like reading, drawing, or talking to a friend. Play a game or exercise to give your brain a break.

3. **Stay connected.** Talk in person whenever possible. Have a voice call, do a video conference, send a text, post on social media, or do anything else you can think of to connect with your friends and family. Virtual connections help when you're not able to connect in person.

> **TRY IT!** Reach out to one different person each day this week.

Three ways to take care of your spirit:

1. **Interact with beauty.** This could be doing something creative yourself (writing, drawing, cooking, singing, rapping, journaling) or stopping to appreciate something beautiful. Go outside and watch the clouds roll past. Look up some art in books or online. Listen to music that really moves you. God's gifts to us are abundant and accessible even in a time of distress.

> **TRY IT!** Take a picture of something beautiful every day for a week and send it to a friend.

2. **Journal.** At the end of the day, jot down what you're grateful for and why. Record humor or points of joy that you had with family or friends. Write down what you're hoping and praying for. Doodle and draw just for fun. If you found beauty in people, art, or nature today, write about how it made you feel.

3. **Pray.** You can talk with God anytime and anywhere. **1 JOHN 5:14** (GNT) says, "We have courage in God's presence, because we are sure that he hears us." Sometimes it helps to write your prayers down to think about what you want to say. But prayer doesn't have to be formal or complicated. You can talk to God like you would talk to any other person.

BOX BREATHING

When our feelings are getting the best of us, one of the most important things we can do is to ground ourselves with our breathing. Practicing deep breathing can help us relieve stress and improve our focus. Once our bodies and our brains are calm, we can choose how we want to move forward in a healthy way.

Slowing and regulating our breathing helps slow our heart rate and lower our blood pressure. This will quiet feelings of panic or high stress and slow the amount of stress hormones that are making us feel on edge and keeping us amped up.

One way to do this is through simple box breathing.

TRY IT! Place your finger at the top left corner of the box. Slowly move your finger to the right as you inhale and count to four. Then hold your breath for four seconds as you move your finger to the bottom right of the square. As you move your finger to the left, exhale for four seconds. Then rest as you move your finger up to complete the square. Do this multiple times to allow your brain and body to get in sync with your breath.

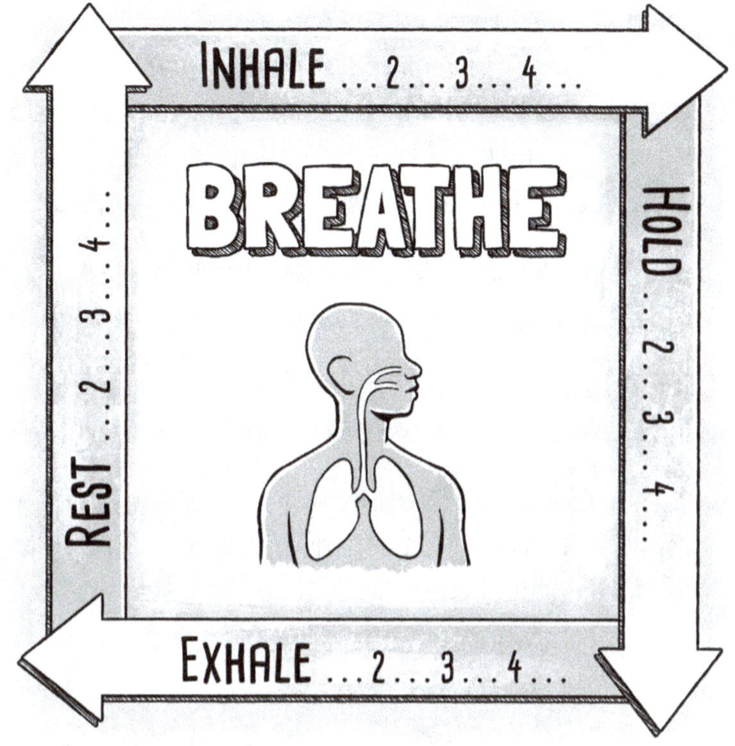

Once you have slowed your breathing, be still for a few minutes. Close your eyes and continue breathing slowly as you think about these words of Jesus: "Peace I leave with you; my peace I give to you. . . . Let not your hearts be troubled, neither let them be afraid." (**JOHN 14:27**).

DAVID'S FEELINGS

Have you heard about David from the Bible? He was a musician, warrior, shepherd, king, and poet. He was far from perfect, but he had all of the qualities you would look for in a great leader. The Bible calls him "a man after God's own heart" (**1 SAMUEL 13:14**).

When David was a young teen he went to the battlefield where his brothers were fighting a war. There was an enormous giant of a man on the other side teasing and taunting the Israelites (David's people) and daring anyone to fight. So David volunteered, then fought and killed the giant and helped conquer the rest of the enemy. He was not the kind of guy you would expect to struggle with anything, especially difficult emotions.

But David did struggle with strong feelings. He spent years on the run, hiding in the mountains and living in caves because people were trying to kill him. Many times he was just trying to survive, with no idea what the future held, feeling stuck and helpless.

In **PSALM 69**, David wrote down how he was feeling. He said,

> Save me, O God! The water is up to my neck!
> I am sinking in deep mud, and there is no solid ground;
> I am out in deep water, and the waves are about to drown me.
> I am worn out from calling for help, and my throat is aching.
> I have strained my eyes, looking for your help. (GNT)

Sounds rough. David was so desperate he could do nothing but cry out to God. Have you ever felt hopeless like him? When David was overwhelmed or afraid, he would often write or sing what he was feeling. The book of Psalms has over forty poems like this, called laments (you will learn more about laments in session 4).

David recognized the power of being able to express his feelings. Here are some of the ways David responded to times of strong difficult feelings. Look up each Bible reference and draw a line to match it to the correct response of David. You can use a printed Bible or search the references online (**PSALM 13** is included on page 55).

**Took care of his body and worshiped
God while he was still grieving**

1 SAMUEL 20:41–42

**Wrote poems or songs to express
his feelings**

2 SAMUEL 12:20

**Reaffirmed his friendship and wept with
his best friend**

1 SAMUEL 30:4, 6

**Grieved with his men about their losses
and found his strength in God**

PSALM 13

TALK ABOUT IT

1. Have you been stuck or felt stuck like David? How did you respond?

2. Think about how you're feeling now. Are you more likely to respond to your feelings by talking and praying with a good friend or writing poetry or music to express yourself? Why?

3. How can you find your strength in God?

When Jesus was on earth, he knew his friends were worried about a lot of things, and they were tired of carrying such heaviness in their hearts. One day he said to them,

> Come to me, all of you who are weary and carry heavy burdens, and I will give you rest . . . Let me teach you, because I am humble and gentle at heart, and you will find rest for your souls. **MATTHEW 11:28–29 NLT**

**You can find rest for your soul by letting go of what is worrying you,
and by finding your strength in God like David did.**

Take a Break!

How Can I Get Unstuck?

CONNECTING THROUGH THE CRAZY

Rosa leaned back in her chair, staring at the ceiling fan going around and around. She was done being angry. All she felt now was sad. Her eyes filled with tears as she thought about missing her last chance at a state championship. This had been the year—the year they would've gone all the way. They'd had the perfect team. They were undefeated. Regionals had been just around the corner. Part of her wondered if she was being selfish. *In the big scheme of life, what's a basketball game?* But then she thought of the countless hours she'd practiced, the aches she'd played through, the disappointments she'd grown from, the victories she'd earned, and suddenly her eyes were filling up. Again. Embarrassed, she wiped them for the thousandth time.

At least no one else is here to see this, she thought. Laura had stopped coming over. She'd endured too many awkward silences that Rosa refused to break. Being around other people was so exhausting, anyway.

She had done text and video chats with some of her friends. This included Natalie, who, despite being shot, seemed to be doing surprisingly well. *But Natalie's always upbeat.* Rosa thought. *And she's got her whole family and church supporting her.* Lately, her friend had been hounding her to connect with their basketball coach. Rosa liked Coach Jay a lot, but didn't know if she was ready for more visitors yet.

Connecting with her friends didn't completely change how she was feeling, but at least she wasn't alone in her thoughts. *What's next?* Everyone was saying something different about the shooting. Some people thought the school was overreacting by canceling everything. Others couldn't believe the school wasn't doing more. *Am I going to spend the rest of my life in this room?* she wondered. *What about college? What about—?*

There was a knock at the door. She dabbed at her eyes. "Yeah?"

"Can I come in?" Phoenix asked.

"Yeah, I guess," Rosa answered. Her brother flopped down on the bed.

Almost three years apart and into different things, Rosa and Phoenix had never been close. Rosa knew he wasn't having a good year, but it had been hard to relate because she loved the school so much. After weeks of isolation, Rosa hadn't been able to face the same four walls of her bedroom anymore. She'd started making grilled cheese sandwiches for their lunches. Phoenix was all onboard with someone else making his favorite food. Who knew that cheesy, gooey goodness could make such a great bonding opportunity? Ever since Rosa flipped the first golden square onto Phoenix's plate, they'd been talking more. It was actually . . . nice.

"So, I'm, like, really scared," Phoenix said.

"Wow," said Rosa. "Just laying it out there, huh?"

"I'm serious," said Phoenix. "Everything is so crazy right now. You don't know what everyone is talking about out there. You remember Rob?"

"Yeah. He was one of your best friends," said Rosa. "What happened?"

"He just posted that his school got shut down because of a bomb threat."

Rosa gasped. "Oh no. I *am* sorry, Phoenix. Are you okay? How's Rob?" Phoenix started telling her about his friend and how much he missed him since they stopped going to the same school. Rob's school was closed for two days while the police searched it. Thankfully, they didn't find anything and everyone was back in class. But Rob was shaken up.

As Phoenix spoke, he was surprised to feel a bit better. It helped to get his feelings out and feel like he was being heard. Things didn't seem quite as scary. He finished with the question that had been on his mind for a long time: "So, what's going to happen if there's another shooting?"

"I don't know," Rosa said, her heart hammering at the thought. "But we'll deal with it somehow, and we've got each other, right?"

"Yeah, I guess we do!" said her brother.

Rosa was grateful to listen to Phoenix. It was nice to be trusted with his fears and concerns—it made her feel like she could still do something for someone else even when she felt helpless in her own situation. She had a thought. "You know what I'm stuck on, Phoenix? I'm sad I've missed so many things with my team and my senior year! The hardest part is being so scared of everything that I wonder if I'll ever leave this house again. Sometimes it makes me so mad, but what good does that do?"

Phoenix nodded. "I'm sorry you've missed out on so many things, Rosa. Dad was going on about how good your team was this year." He paused and then smiled. "What do you think about playing a substitute championship game? Just some one-on-one hoops, you and me—winner take . . . *the universe!*" he finished in an announcer voice.

Rosa laughed. "What? Are you kidding? You hate sports!" She tossed a basketball over to him.

Phoenix scrambled for it, then settled back down on the bed. "Yeah, but that's only because I didn't want to show you up with the basketball superpowers I've been hiding all this time." He started laughing, too. "It'll be perfect! We can get mom and dad to dress up like cheerleaders and . . ."

Rosa's sides began to hurt from laughing. Eventually, she caught her breath enough to gasp, "Okay, maybe not for the universe and *definitely* not with mom and dad as cheerleaders, but . . . it'd be nice throwing a ball around with you. If you're up for it."

"Sure."

The doorbell rang. They looked at each other.

"Coach Jay!" Rosa's basketball coach had been concerned about her long absence and decided to check in. That was just like her. She was always volunteering with her church, cleaning up along the highways, and helping out at the food pantry. Her warm smile and some freshly baked cookies kept Phoenix from vanishing into his room. Coach Jay had an easygoing attitude and was easy to talk to. The siblings surprised themselves with how much they both had to say in the hour before she left with a promise to visit again soon. It was a relief to unload some of their feelings with Coach Jay.

Later that evening, Rosa and Phoenix couldn't hold back the laughter as they tried staring each other down during their epic basketball game. It felt good to relax and blow off steam—to feel connected.

1. Why do you think Rosa felt better when she was listening to Phoenix's feelings? Why did they feel relieved to be heard?

2. Why is sharing our stories helpful? What makes sharing our stories difficult?

3. Who do you have in your life that you trust and can talk to? Who can you listen to?

4. What are some physically active things, like playing basketball, that you can do to release the tension you feel?

TELLING YOUR STORY

One of the best ways you can deal with difficult feelings is to talk about them. Telling the story about difficult times in your life can help you feel better. It's best to talk to someone you can trust—ideally, someone you already have a relationship with.

You can get to your story by saying something like, "Hey, I want to talk about something that has been bothering me." Then talk about the circumstances in your life that have made you struggle with difficult feelings. That's your story.

Here's a good way to structure your story. Look at the bullseye target below. Fill in the answers from your own experience to the question on each level:

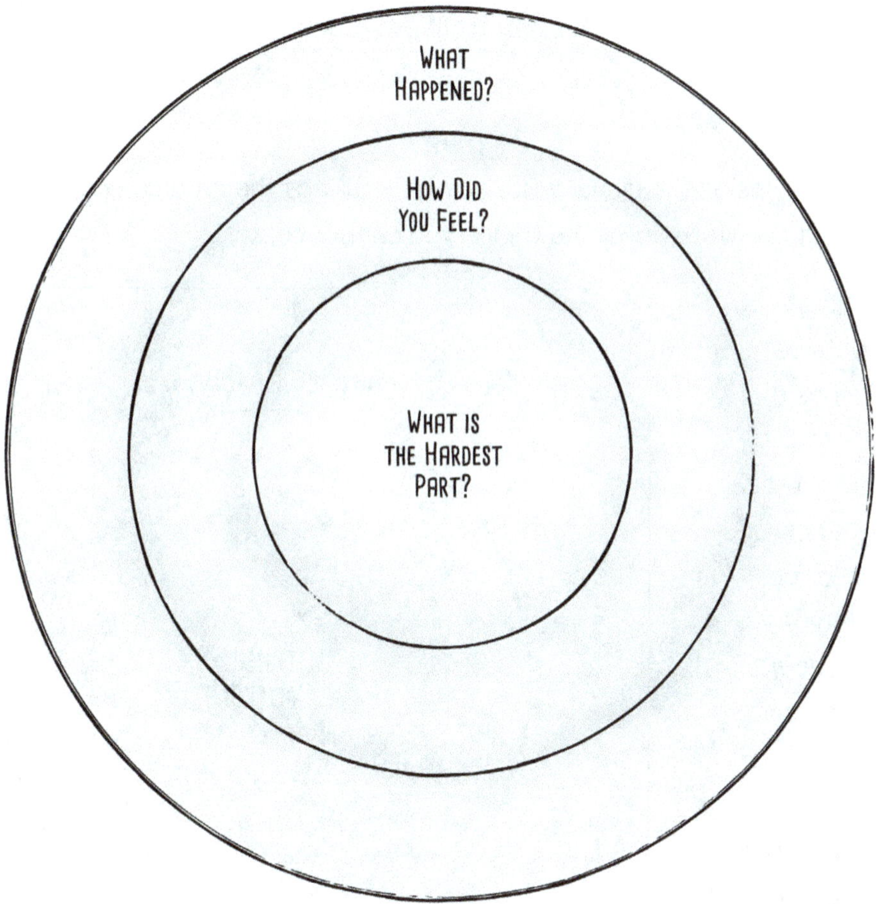

TRY IT! Find someone this week that you can share your story with. It's best to start with a small story, not the hardest thing you've been through. Afterward, you could help your friends or family members by being a good listener. Ask them these three questions about a small story of their own. Remember, being a good listener does not mean trying to "fix" people or solve their problems.

CIRCLE OF CONTROL

In uncertain times, things can feel chaotic, like everything is out of control. The anxiety of not knowing how things will turn out and how long the chaos will last can feel overwhelming.

When you are feeling overwhelmed, it can be helpful to pause and look at what you can and cannot control right now, in this specific moment. This can help you let go of those things that are not in your control and help you feel empowered to focus on the things you can control. This exercise can ground you in the present moment and give you something practical to do.

For example, you might not be able to control the actions of others and how they are responding to this crisis, but you *can* control how you are responding. You cannot control how long things will feel in a crisis mode, but you *can* control your attitude and find positive things to do today.

Look at the circle. Inside the circle, write down the things that you can control. On the outside of the circle, write down the things you cannot control.

Notice the things you wrote outside the circle, things that you can't control. It's likely that these are things that cause you to worry or be stressed out in other ways. What if you were able to give those things to God? Take a moment to ask God to calm your heart and help you let go of the things you can't control.

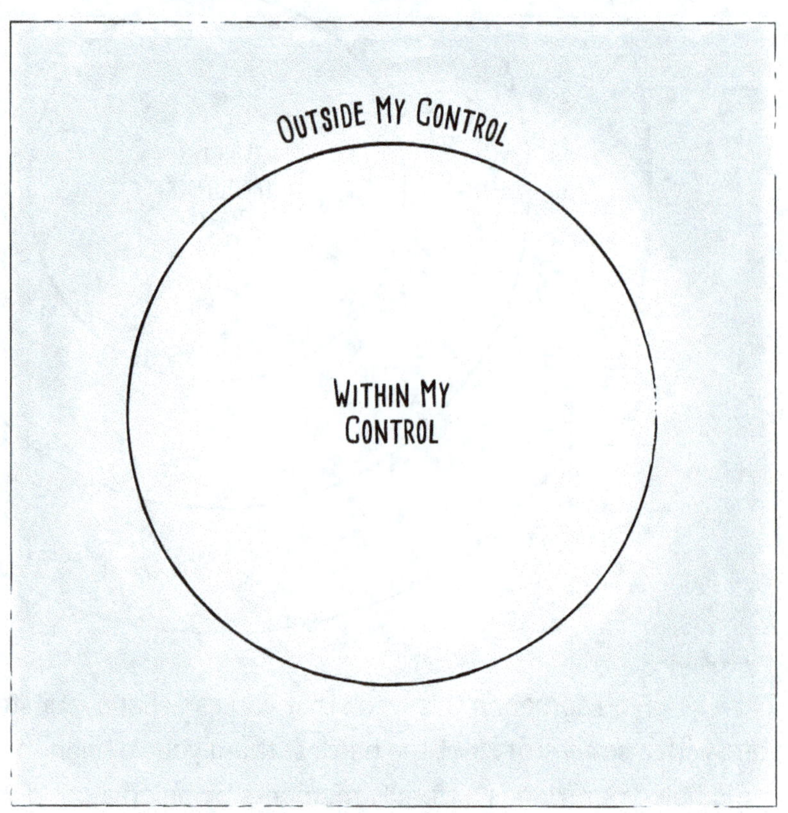

MAP YOUR GOALS

Before your life was interrupted by this crisis, what were some of your goals for the future? What were you working toward, dreaming of, planning for, or counting on happening? You may feel all these things are impossible now, or doubt that you'll ever reach your goals.

But if you take steps toward those goals, no matter how small, you will begin to feel unstuck. One way to organize your thinking about your goals for the future is to make a kind of map. Follow these steps on the next page:

1. Start in the middle box and write your name or draw a picture of yourself.

2. Choose your goal categories and write them into the ovals. They might include things like Create, Health, Fun, Travel, People, Hobbies, Job, Family, Mind, Save Money.

3. Draw lines coming out of each oval and write things you can do to reach your goal. Include the easiest, smallest things you can do, and a few of the more difficult steps you'll need to take.

You might want to create this map on a separate piece of paper and hang it on your wall to encourage and remind yourself to keep moving toward your goals. It will make you feel less stuck to feel movement and accomplishment, no matter how small.

In **PROVERBS 16:9** in the Bible, a wise man said, "We can make our plans, but the LORD determines our steps." And, in **PROVERBS 3:5–6** it says, "Trust in the LORD with all your heart; do not depend on your own understanding. Seek his will in all you do, and he will show you which path to take" (NLT).

Take a moment to ask God for his help and guidance in moving toward your goals.

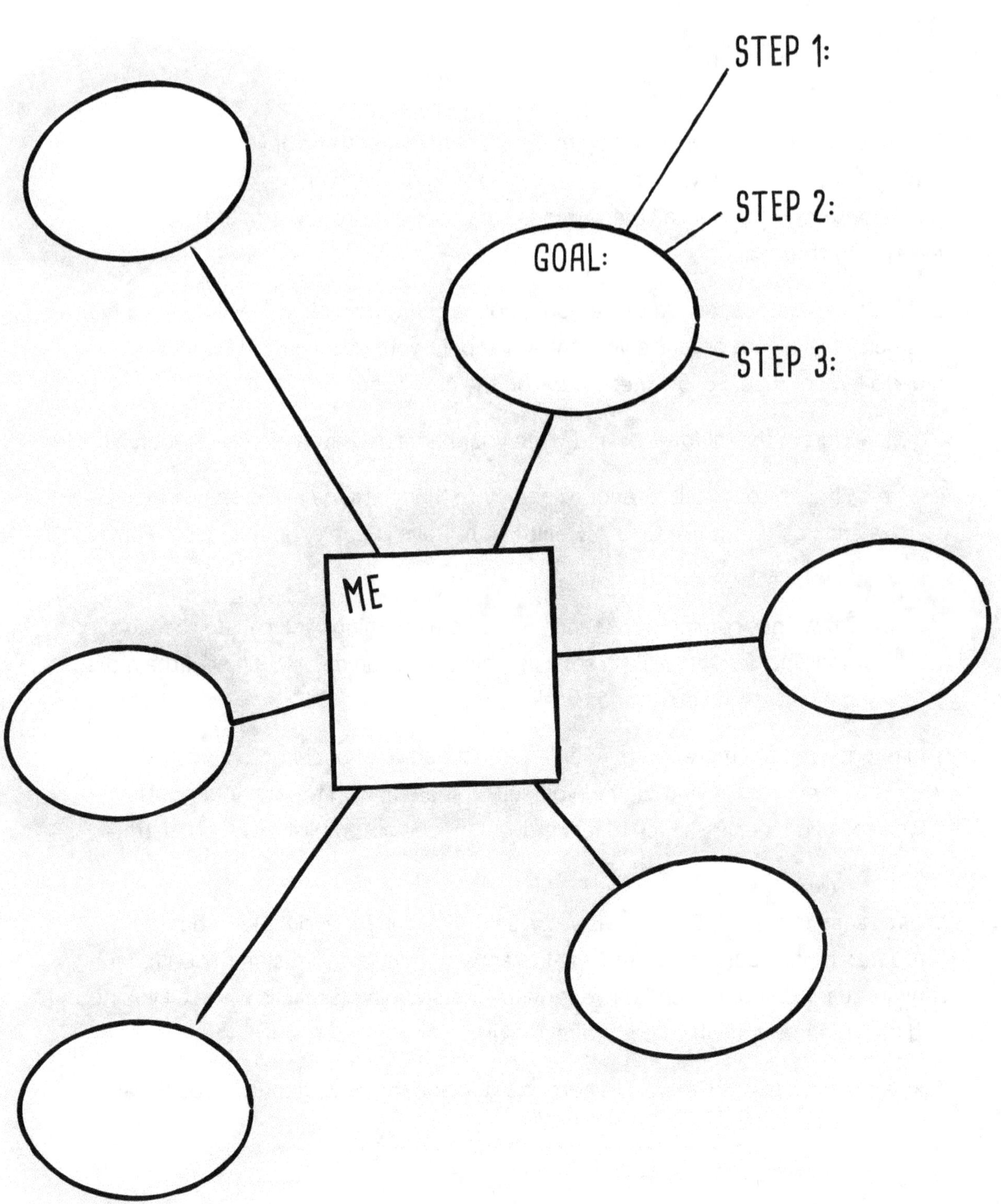

STEP 1:
STEP 2:
GOAL:
STEP 3:
ME

THE NEXT GOOD THING

When the immediate needs of a crisis are met and you are struggling to bring your life back to normal, you may feel lost, unsure what to do next, and sometimes totally bored. This can feel terrible. But it is also an incredible opportunity. It can trigger your imagination to create or try something new! It can motivate you to do things you've always wanted to do. It can be a time for refreshment and open your eyes to wider possibilities. If you're feeling overwhelmed, do something simple that you know is good.

TRY IT! See how many of these suggestions you can check off over the next several weeks.

☐ Write a note to encourage a friend or family member.
Even better, put it on paper and mail it!

☐ Draw or paint a picture.

☐ Learn a new skill or strengthen an existing one—drawing, hair braiding, guitar playing, building a garden. What else? Try an online tutorial to start.

☐ Clean your room—no, really: turn on some music and jump in.
Your space affects your feelings.

☐ Read a book—get lost in someone else's story.

☐ Do something physically tiring—run the stairs,
do jumping jacks, whatever gets you moving.

☐ Get outside. Take a walk. Take a run. Sit under a tree.
Listen to running water or watch the waves.

☐ Be curious about something you notice and learn as much as you can about that thing—caterpillars are cool. Stars are beautiful. How do they make cheese puffs?

☐ Write a story—get in your head and find a story there.

☐ Do a puzzle—perfect with music and hot chocolate.

☐ Make a batch of cookies.

☐ Cook dinner for your family—find a new favorite recipe.

☐ Find a way to volunteer your help—the world needs your gifts.

☐ Take responsibility for improving one room in the house in some way—big or small.

☐ Plan a family hike—if you can, where you can, when you can.

☐ Plan the road trip of a lifetime—you can go anywhere in your imagination.

☐ Organize the pictures on your phone—you have to do it sometime.

☐ Ask someone to play a game—online or where you're staying, what'll it be?

☐ Make a list of the things and people you are thankful for—yes, shoelaces and backpacks count. How many can you come up with?

____

____

____

____

____

____

____

____

____

____

____

____

____

____

LISTENING WITH JOB

One of the great things about the Bible is that it gives us stories about both good and bad behavior. This story is a summary of the book of Job (**JOB 1—3, 16, 38—42**). How do the people in Job's story do at listening well?

Job was a really awesome guy. He loved God and lived a good moral life. He was loaded; he had money, massive estates, many animals, lots of people working for him, a big family, and the full respect of his community. However, there came a moment in his life when everything changed. God allowed Satan to test Job and see what was important to him. Job lost everything in one day: all of his children and wealth and servants—everything but his house and his wife.

Then it got worse. He got sick and his body was covered with sores and scabs. As he was sitting there in pain and grief, his wife said to him, "Why don't you curse God and die?" But Job answered, "Don't talk like a fool! If we accept blessings from God, we must accept trouble as well." Job never once said anything against God.

At this point, his three friends Eliphaz, Bildad, and Zophar come to visit. They barely recognize him. First, they cry with Job. Then they sit with him without saying anything. After a full week of being quiet together, Job breaks the silence. He curses—not God, but the day he was born. He longs for death. He complains to God.

Then Eliphaz speaks up. He tells Job that his pain is because of his own sin and he needs to repent. Bildad and Zophar agree that Job must have done evil things and that's why he's suffering. They even say that his children brought destruction on themselves and deserved it, and that Job must have done something to deserve this punishment, as well. They talk a lot. They quote wise sayings.

Eventually Job tells them they're "miserable comforters" and wishes they would shut up. His friends came to comfort him but they only made his suffering worse. However wise their sayings, they don't apply to him. He's innocent.

At one point, Job complains to Eliphaz that he wishes he could make his case directly to God instead of to his friends. God would be a better listener:

> Would God use all his strength against me?
> No, he would listen as I spoke.
>
> **JOB 23:6 GNT**

Job complains a lot more. Finally, Job asks God to explain what is happening. And God responds, but not by explaining. Instead, God asks Job questions. "Why do you talk so much when you know so little? Were you there when I made the world? How large is

---

the earth? Can you arrange stars in groups like Orion? Can you order the clouds to send a downpour? Can you make a wild ox work for you? Did you give the horse its strength and its flowing mane?"

God asks Job question after question, showing the difference in power, viewpoint, and wisdom between God and Job. Finally Job answers God. "I have talked about things that are beyond my understanding." And somehow Job is satisfied. He stops complaining.

But God was angry with Job's friends because they thought they knew why Job was suffering. They had said things about God that were not true. God tells Eliphaz that *they* are the ones who deserve punishment. They must bring a sacrifice and Job will pray for them. God will listen to Job's prayer and forgive the friends. After this, God blessed Job with ten new children and twice as much land and animals as he had before. He lived to an old age and saw his great-grandchildren.

TALK ABOUT IT

1. What did Job's listeners do that was helpful? What did they do that was not helpful?

2. How do God's questions help Job think about his suffering?

3. Who was God angry with? Why?

4. If you or people you know have had a similar experience, how did others respond to their pain?

5. What questions do you have for God? What questions might God have for you?

HOW DOES GOD LISTEN?

The rest of the Bible agrees with Job that God is a good and patient listener! God was not angry with Job for asking hard questions. The Bible tells us a lot about how God listens to us. Check out these Bible verses. Can you see any patterns?

> You will listen, O LORD, to the prayers of the lowly;
> you will give them courage.
> **PSALM 10:17 GNT**

> You are good to us and forgiving,
> full of constant love for all who pray to you.
> **PSALM 86:5 GNT**

But God has indeed heard me;
he has listened to my prayer.
I praise God, because he did not reject my prayer
or keep back his constant love from me.   **PSALM 66:19–20 GNT**

I call to the LORD for help;
I plead with him.
I bring him all my complaints;
I tell him all my troubles.   **PSALM 142:1–2 GNT**

He is near to those who call to him,
who call to him with sincerity.   **PSALM 145:18 GNT**

God is both powerful and patient. He is ready to listen to you.

TAKE A BREAK!

What Is Happening Inside of Me?

LIFE ON A HAIR TRIGGER

Daniel was caught up in the basketball game his sister was playing and didn't see Tyler making his way toward him through the crowded stands.

Daniel's friend Sam started elbowing him. "Daniel. Daniel. Dude—*Daniel!*"

Daniel looked over just in time to see a scowling Tyler come up on him and pull back a fist.

"Gun!" someone shouted over the noise of the game. There was a scream and a gunshot boomed across the school gym. To Daniel, it sounded like it had gone off right by his ear. People were jumping over seats and falling over benches in their attempts to get away. It was chaos. His heart felt like it was punching out of his chest. Everyone was pushing and pushing. It wasn't until he was halfway across the parking lot that he recovered enough to think, *Did Tyler just try to kill me? Where's Sam?* "Wait—Natalie!"

He checked his phone and saw the missed calls and panicked texts from his parents. They had been at the game too, but he and Sam were on the other side of the gym. He was shocked to learn his sister had been grazed by a bullet.

"Where were you?" demanded his dad once Daniel caught up with them. "I know it was crazy in there, but your mom and I made it down to the court as soon as we saw Natalie on the floor."

"Dad, I—I didn't know!" He felt his face grow red. "I just . . . ran, I guess. I just did what everyone else did."

"You ran," his dad said flatly. "You ran while your sister lay bleeding on the court. She could have been dead, Daniel!"

"I know," he said miserably. "I'm sorry."

His dad's face softened. "I'm sorry I reacted like that, son." He placed his hands on Daniel's shoulders and looked him in the eye. "You're right—in a situation like that, running makes sense. I'm glad you're safe."

Aside from a few scrapes and bruises, no one else was seriously hurt. The shooting took place after official hours, so the school reopened a few days later. They canceled extracurricular activities for the rest of the year, though.

When Daniel apologized to his sister for running out on her, Natalie just smiled. "Don't worry about it, Dan. Yeah, it's been rough going, but you couldn't have done anything. It's cool."

But it wasn't cool. He felt ashamed. His sleep was broken with nightmares of his sister dying, him dying, or both of them dying. He kept having terrible stomach cramps. Worse, he felt responsible for what happened.

Tyler had tormented Daniel for a long time. Until recently, that is, when Daniel had finally told someone about it and gotten Tyler suspended for a week. He'd felt blindsided when Tyler suddenly showed up in front of him at the game, looking like he wanted payback for his suspension. Daniel was convinced that whoever had shouted "Gun!" must have seen Tyler holding one. He thought the shot was aimed at him.

But Sam said Tyler didn't have a gun at all. Sam thought someone else's drama was playing out next to them just when Tyler showed up. "I think you just freaked out," his friend said the next day. "Everything blew up all at once, and you started seeing things." A couple days later, Sam seemed to be proven right when the police reported they had arrested someone else for the incident.

Daniel was relieved he wasn't the cause of the shooting, but he couldn't shrug off what happened that night or how he responded by running away. Plus, he still felt targeted. Tyler's suspension was about up and he was due back in school soon. Daniel was terrified of running into him again. *Okay, maybe he didn't want to kill me, but he definitely wanted some serious revenge.* It was inevitable: they were going to meet sooner or later.

He grabbed his bedroom door and slammed it back against the wall again and again until the doorknob had made a sizable hole. No one yelled—the house was empty. It matched his feelings. "What am I going to do?" he whispered.

It was morning. His parents had left for work. Natalie's friends had already picked her up for school. Daniel had said he'd rather walk. Now he sat on his parents' bed, looking at the handgun in his dad's nightstand drawer. It seemed he sat there a long time. He finally got up, went to the kitchen, and filled a small glass from the liquor cabinet. He grimaced as it went down. After thoroughly cleaning the glass, he went back into his parents' bedroom.

The gun was heavier than he expected. He kept thinking it would go off in his hands. He placed it carefully in his backpack. *It's just for protection*, he reassured himself. *Maybe I'll just scare him a little, so he'll back off.*

✳   ✳   ✳

In the school hallway, balloons hovered over the stream of teens. Somebody's birthday. Daniel scanned the crowded corridor. The extra weight in his pack pulled at him— seemed to slow his steps. Up ahead, Tyler was opening his locker. Usually, Daniel avoided this hall. Now, he slid the pack off his shoulder and started unzipping the pocket. His head hurt and his heart was racing.

BANG!

People screamed, and everyone in the hall hit the floor, including Daniel. Someone was laughing. "Guys, relax—it was just a balloon!" Everyone sighed in one shaky breath. Some began to chuckle. A girl was yelling at the kid who'd pulled the prank.

And Daniel was out the door, throwing up in the bushes. He was trembling. Even knowing it was only a balloon, he felt just as he had when the gunshot had echoed through the gym. He thought about what he'd been about to do, and suddenly he just wanted to go home. *Yay, look at me, Dad,* he thought. *Running makes complete sense, right?*

"Hey, are you okay?"

Daniel jumped. The basketball coach was looking at him with concern. What was her name? Janna? No, *Janya*. But everyone called her Coach Jay. He remembered she had a rep for being involved with her church and helping out around town. His sister was a big fan. In fact, Natalie had been attending her coach's church for a while now.

Coach Jay walked toward him, and he felt fear again, thinking about the gun in his backpack. "Class is about to start," she said, "but you don't look like you're feeling well."

"Yeah," he gave a sickly smile. "I don't think I'm up for class right now."

"You're Natalie's brother, aren't you?"

"Yeah."

"I thought so. I came by to visit her the other day, but I must have missed you." Coach Jay hesitated, then continued. "I know it's been a rough week. Sometimes it can help to talk things out."

"Maybe." Daniel felt tears gathering. He looked down, hoping they wouldn't fall and embarrass him even more. "But not just now, I think."

"Fair enough." Jay nodded. "I'll be by your place again tomorrow afternoon to see your sister. Will you be there?"

Daniel wiped his eyes. "Yeah."

Coach Jay smiled. "Good. I'd like to talk some more, if you're open to it."

"Yeah, okay." It felt good to admit it—to admit wanting—*needing*—to talk. His heart slowed a bit. His breathing eased. The world suddenly didn't seem quite so lonely.

Coach Jay led him toward the hallway. "I'm going to write you an excuse for today, but before I do, I want to leave you with a thought. When I'm going through dark times, it helps me to remember that God is a shelter and strength, always ready to help in times of trouble." [**PSALM 46:1**]

"Okay." Daniel slowly nodded his head. He didn't quite get it, but the words stuck with him for the rest of the day.

Later, before his parents got home, he returned the gun to the nightstand. 

💬 TALK ABOUT IT

1. What is Daniel feeling? Why do you think he is feeling that way?

2. How did he respond? What are some other ways he could have responded?

3. What happened when the balloon popped? What was Daniel's reaction?

4. How can you relate to the story with the things you have felt or experienced in your own life?

HIDING OUR FEELINGS

*(**Groups:** Before the session, prepare several empty water bottles with lids, along with a bucket of water. And maybe a towel! **On your own:** See the video linked on page 62.)*

Everyone has feelings. God created us to respond with feelings to our life experiences—and to our memories. There are many kinds of feelings: easily named ones like *angry, sad,* and *happy,* and more complex ones like *confused, frustrated, content,* or *depressed.* When we're not ready to handle difficult feelings, we often try to hide them from others.

Groups: Share some of the feelings we tend to hide inside, like shame, fear, frustration, and so on. As you share, write these feelings on the bottles with a marker (or write them on slips of paper and put the papers in the bottles).

Put the bottles in the water one by one as you talk together. Have a volunteer try and keep all the bottles under the water with one hand (not forearm).

As you will discover, it's not possible to keep more than a few bottles under water at the same time.

In the same way, keeping our feelings inside takes a lot of energy and attention. The feelings end up coming out in unexpected ways—like explosive anger or depression (remember the volcano activity?). These behaviors can be destructive to ourselves and other people. It's best to express our feelings in healthy ways rather than trying to hold them inside.

💬 TALK ABOUT IT

1. Can you think of a time when you or someone close to you tried to hide some feelings? How long did they stay hidden? What happened?

2. What are some healthy ways you can express your feelings instead of hiding them?

HOW OUR BRAINS REACT TO DANGER

Did you know that God made you with instincts? Your body is ready to respond quickly and automatically when stressful things happen to you, just like you pull your hand back fast when you touch something hot.

One way to summarize how our brain works in cases of stress is this: we have an "upstairs brain" and a "downstairs brain," connected by a flight of stairs.

The **upstairs brain** is where we do our thinking and decision making. It is where our memories are stored.

The **downstairs brain** regulates the bodily functions that happen without our thinking about them—our heartbeat, breathing, and other things that keep us alive. It's also responsible for our reflexes and our instincts—especially the survival instinct. The downstairs brain doesn't take time to think like the upstairs brain, so it responds faster.

The connecting flight of stairs is the **midbrain**. The midbrain notices the emotions our body is feeling and communicates them to the downstairs and upstairs brains.

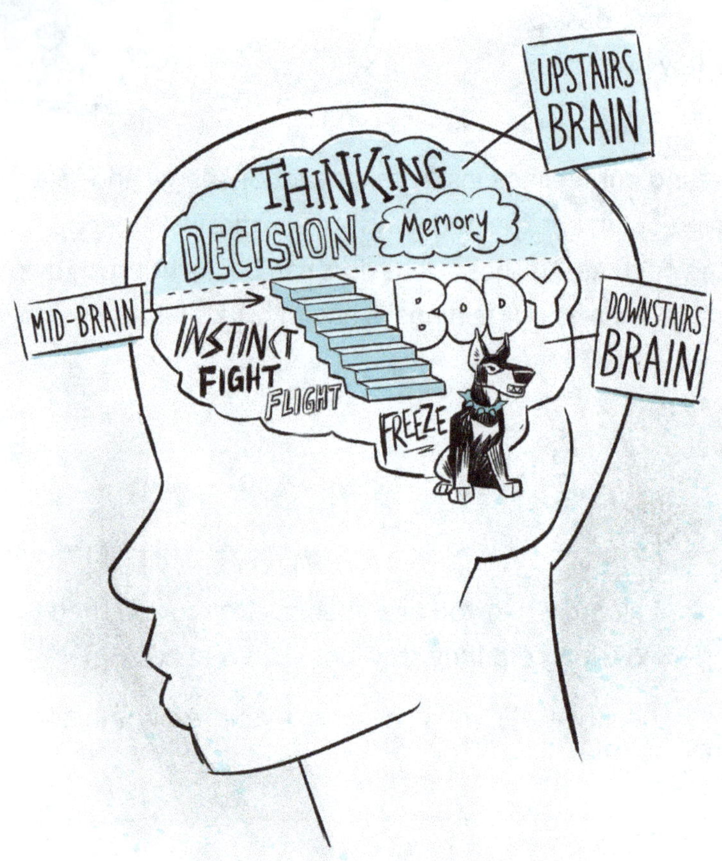

A **watchdog** lives in the downstairs brain. It's a survival function, warning us when there's danger. The watchdog prompts us to respond by redirecting our energies—and interrupting normal brain activity. It reacts quickly, but it has a limited range of responses. It prepares us either to fight the danger, to run away from it, or to shut down entirely. We call this the "fight, flight, or freeze" response.

- When we face a dangerous or stressful situation, our "downstairs brain" reacts more quickly than our "upstairs brain."
- Sometimes these reactions help us escape real danger, but often our automatic reactions are too strong or don't fit the situation.
- When we're using only our survival instinct, it can be hard to think well or make good decisions.
- If we experience a lot of stress over a long period, our inner watchdog may start to "bark" even when there's no immediate danger.

When the watchdog alerts you to the fight-flight-freeze response on a **false alarm**, your upstairs brain, the thinking part, can usually quiet the watchdog by telling it that there is no danger and there is no need to respond.

MY STRESS RESPONSES

The watchdog's response can take our upstairs brain offline for a while. If you know how you normally respond to stress, it is easier to recognize when that happens. And that can help you hold on long enough for your upstairs brain to catch up—and come up with a better response. Here are some ways to identify these three responses to stress:

FIGHT

- Raising your voice
- Arguing
- Kicking or screaming
- Tightening muscles
- Clenching fist

FLIGHT

- Running away
- Restless body
- Rapid breathing, pounding heart
- Feeling trapped
- Excessive exercise

FREEZE

- Holding your breath
- Disconnected from feelings
- Unable to talk or make decisions
- Feeling like you can't move
- Tuning out, daydreaming
- Feeling numb

Look at the scenarios below. Which part of the brain—upstairs or downstairs—is in control for each of the people? Which fight, flight, or freeze response does each one demonstrate?

1. John is riding his bike when he is hit by a car and thrown onto the street. He is bleeding and he lifts up his bike and throws it at the car. Now he's running around screaming and cussing at the driver of the car that hit him.

2. Sarah is in her room. She hears her parents screaming at each other and throwing things across the house. She sits on her bed, staring out the window.

3. Kevin was abused by his uncle. When it happened, he took off running. Now every time the uncle comes around everything inside him wants to run away again, and sometimes he does.

TALK ABOUT IT

1. Which of the three survival responses do you use when you're stressed? How do you show that reaction?

2. Which ones have you seen in other people—family members, close friends?

3. How could it help to know how you or your family members respond to stress or danger?

TRIGGERS

Anything that reminds us of a memory, event, or person in the past is called a trigger. The smell of dinner cooking could fill us with warm memories of our grandmother. Hearing a dog bark could remind us of the time the neighbor's dog bit our hand.

When we're struggling with stress or experiencing trauma, triggers can act like a trigger on a gun and our mind's attention is hit with a painful memory. Immediately, the watchdog at the bottom of the stairs alerts us to danger *from that past event.* Even when there is no danger right now, our survival response takes over. It takes good thinking by the upstairs brain to calm ourselves down.

Triggers can be made less powerful if we take the sting out of the memories connected with them—that is, if we can reduce the associated emotional pain by expressing it in healthy ways, including sharing our story over time with a trusted listener.

Do you have triggers that set off memories of something that happened—good or bad?

TASTE

SIGHT

SMELL

SOUND

TOUCH

TALK ABOUT IT

1. What do you think will happen if you try to avoid your triggers?

2. What are some unhealthy ways people deal with pain? What are some healthy ways people can deal with their pain? What activities have you learned from other sessions that could be helpful here?

COLOR YOUR PAIN

Use this space, or a separate sheet of paper. Take a few minutes to get in touch with the pain and other feelings you have experienced due to loss. Use color, design, and abstract or concrete symbols to represent each kind of feeling as it comes to your awareness. Don't overthink! Stop after five minutes or so and see what you've been able to capture on paper. If you're in a group, consider talking about your artwork with them. If not, think about someone you can share this with.

A RANGE OF FEELINGS

The poems in the book of Psalms express the whole range of human emotions. They include laments along with songs of celebration, encouragement, and hope. Look at a few of these verses. Can you name the feelings described?

Verse (NLT)		Emotion
PSALM 25:16	. . . I am alone and in deep distress.	1.
PSALM 18:1	I love you, LORD; you are my strength.	2.
PSALM 31:10	I am dying from grief; my years are shortened by sadness.	3.
PSALM 38:18	But I confess my sins; I am deeply sorry for what I have done.	4.
PSALM 42:5	Why am I discouraged? Why is my heart so sad?	5.
PSALM 44:15	We can't escape the constant humiliation; shame is written across our faces.	6.
PSALM 4:7	You have given me greater joy than those who have abundant harvests of grain and new wine.	7.
PSALM 4:8	In peace I will lie down and sleep, for you alone, O LORD, will keep me safe.	8.
PSALM 6:7	My vision is blurred by grief . . .	9.
PSALM 33:22	Let your unfailing love surround us, LORD, for our hope is in you alone.	10.
PSALM 55:5	Fear and trembling overwhelm me, and I can't stop shaking.	11.
PSALM 35:18	Then I will thank you in front of the great assembly. I will praise you before all the people.	12.

TAKE A BREAK!

Key: 1. Lonely, worried; 2. Love, confidence; 3. Sorrow, depression, sadness, grief; 4. Regret, remorse, repentance; 5. Discouragement, sorrow; 6. Shame, embarrassment; 7. Happiness, joy, satisfaction; 8. Peace, security; 9. Sorrow, grief, overwhelm; 10. Hope; 11. Overwhelmed, fearful; 12. Gratitude.

How Can I Relate to God in Uncertain Times?

ELEVATE THE COMPLAINT

Rosa and Phoenix began to look forward to Coach Jay's weekly visits. Rosa had always liked Jay's personable mentoring style on the basketball court. Now she was growing to appreciate her coach's ability to put words to some of the feelings and challenges she and Phoenix faced. When Jay was a child, her family had fled here as war refugees. Rosa wondered if that was why the coach seemed better than other adults at picking up on what she and Phoenix were experiencing.

Coach Jay managed all the school's basketball teams, and she saw that many players were struggling like Rosa and Phoenix. She invited all the students—players and nonplayers—to hang out once a week at the community center. Phoenix pestered Rosa out of the house so they could go together. It helped that Rosa's friend Natalie was part of the group. Phoenix began connecting with a couple of gamers from the freshman basketball team. It was nice to be with other teens again. Each week, Jay and a leader from her church had an activity to help them learn to cope with their situation.

Sometimes they would play games. A few times they tried different ways to help the teens talk about the shooting and how they were feeling. This week they had a question-and-answer activity. People wrote down questions before the meeting for Coach Jay to answer when they were together. Phoenix had asked: "I don't know if I believe in a God, but if there is one, where is he in all this?"

Jay nodded when she read his note. "That's a great question, Phoenix. When terrible events happen, it's natural for people to start asking what it all means. I believe there is a God and that when he created the world, he made it perfect, without any suffering—no war, no diseases, and no violence."

"So, what happened?" Natalie's brother Daniel asked. "Has God just been tuning out since then or something?"

"No," Jay smiled. "God gave humans a choice to live his way or choose our own way. In the beginning of God's story—in the Bible—when Adam and Eve chose their own way, they disobeyed God. Because of that, suffering entered the world. Now all the earth suffers. The Bible even says, 'For we know that up to the present time all of creation groans with pain.'" [ROMANS 8:22]

"But here's the key," Jay said. "Even in the middle of all this mess, and even though we all disobey God, he has promised never to leave us or forsake us." [HEBREWS 13:5]

Rosa frowned. "Okay, that's nice and all, but what does it mean for us now?"

Natalie spoke up. "For me, it means that even though I can feel so alone in scary times and I don't know the future, I know God is with me and loves me—no matter what."

Coach Jay was nodding again. "I like that, Nat! I hope that thought has been especially comforting for you lately." She paused for a moment. "You know, one word picture in the Bible I like to think of is that God is like a fortress that I can run to for shelter. [PSALM 18:2] I feel like my relationship with Jesus is that place where I can find hope when I am afraid. And that reminds me of something we can do. God encourages us to talk to him about our problems. One way to do that is with a lament.

"A lament is a complaint to God," Jay continued. "The Bible is full of them. It might sound weird, but this kind of complaint is a healthy way to talk to God about the difficult things we experience. God already knows what we are going through, but it helps us to be completely honest with him and say exactly how we are feeling instead of pretending everything is fine.

"I've written laments before, and they have helped me. I have a handout with information about how to create a lament if you want to give it a try. We can talk more about this next week and—no pressure—but maybe some of you will want to share your laments with the rest of us."

As they walked home, Rosa and Phoenix talked about what Coach Jay had said. Rosa had an idea. "Hey, let's write one and test it on each other."

"Okay, but you can't laugh at mine!" said Phoenix.

"I won't if you won't," said Rosa. "Anyway, why not give it a shot?" They went to their rooms to check out Coach Jay's handout and work on their laments.

The next morning, they shared what they had written with each other. Rosa read hers first:

I don't get it, God. I don't get what's happening in the world. I don't get what's happening to me. Everything's trashed. What do I do? Am I going to be alright? Are you real? Do you care? How could you let someone nearly kill me for no reason? Can you hear me? Is my heart loud enough for you? Help me out here, okay? I just need to get through this somehow. I need to know someone's looking out for me. Will you?

Phoenix had made a detailed drawing of himself. His mouth was wide open in a shout, or maybe a scream. It was about five times as big as the rest of his head. Between teeth the size of cinder blocks, he had written these words:

> *Okay, God, what's up? How's it all so messed up?*
> *My world is shook up, like it's 'bout to blow up.*
> *Is it a set up? When you plan to show up?*
> *Need you to speak up, before I just give up.*
> *Bad to get worked up, but now I can't shut up,*
> *So won't you step up—stand and be my backup?*

Rosa and Phoenix sat in silence for a few minutes thinking about their laments. It helped to lay out their feelings to God. They still did not know how long they were going to feel on edge or if they would be safe. But somehow things seemed a little bit different. By trying out the things they were learning and helping each other, maybe they could get through this uncertain time together. Maybe they could feel a little more . . . unstuck.

Rosa traced the lines of Phoenix's drawing with her finger. "I like what Coach Jay said," she murmured. "When it comes to my fears and stuff, I kinda do feel like God could be my fortress and shield."

"Yeah." Phoenix looked thoughtful. "Maybe."

1. What do you think Coach Jay meant when she said that having a relationship with Jesus makes her feel less afraid?

2. Why is it helpful to tell God exactly what we're feeling?

3. Why are things starting to feel different to Rosa and Phoenix now than they did in the beginning of this story?

4. Are you feeling different now about your situation than you did when you started these lessons? Why or why not?

GRIEF STREET

You have likely experienced loss. The feelings you have named are connected to the grief you're feeling because of those losses. Loss always leads to grief. Grief is the emotional response we feel when we have lost someone or something. Grief is normal and healthy, as it helps us deal with our loss.

Grief is a process. Our losses are different, but we all take a similar journey in dealing with them. Everyone goes through stages of grief. Each stage is a necessary part of the grieving process. Sometimes we go back to an earlier stage for a while. Sometimes we get stuck and need help. But there's no way to bypass the journey.

We can think of our grief journey as a street with bus stops along the way.

Bus Stop 1: DENIAL & ANGER

Often our first response to losing something or someone important is denial, to not believe it is possible. Along with doubting that it's true, we sometimes feel numb, with no emotions at all. Often we feel angry about the loss and try to find someone or something to blame so we can aim our anger there. Sometimes anger feels better than feeling numb, and sometimes we can feel safer to express anger than to express our sorrow.

Bus Stop 2: NO HOPE

Eventually, our denial and anger fade, and we face the reality of the loss, causing us to feel hopeless, as if nothing will ever be good again. Some people show this stage by crying, withdrawing, or being depressed. You may not feel like taking care of yourself or doing schoolwork. You may feel like numbing the pain with activities that are harmful to you. Sometimes, people cover up their true feelings in this stage by pretending that everything is okay, that it "doesn't matter."

Bus Stop 3: NEW BEGINNINGS

This is a place of resolution, where we recognize that things will never be the same but we can learn to live with the loss. We can talk about our loss without the sharp pain that we felt when the loss was new. We accept that we can't get those things or people back, and we are able to accept a "new normal" in the face of the loss.

Grief Street Bypass

Sometimes people want to skip all the stops and try to take a bypass directly to New Beginnings. They don't allow themselves the time or space to be sad or angry about their loss. Maybe there are people in their lives who tell them to "just get over it." Or people might say that they should "praise God for everything all the time." The Bypass is not healthy. Going through the stages of grief is important so we can deal with our loss honestly and get to New Beginnings in a natural way.

Riding the Bus

Often the grief journey is not direct. Many times when you think about something or someone you have lost, you find your feelings going back to a stage you thought you had already passed. You might go back to anger (Bus Stop 1), or feeling hopelessness (Bus Stop 2). Over time, and sometimes with help from a friend or safe adult, you are able to move forward again, eventually coming to stay in New Beginnings.

If you did this a group, you could draw the journey and as a group share some ways you would feel (or have felt) at those bus stops. Or try drawing your own version of Grief Street and the three stops.

TRY IT. Look back at your list of losses from Session 1. Decide what stage of grief you're feeling for each one, and write those losses next to the appropriate bus stop in your drawing or the Grief Street graphic above. For example, if you're feeling angry about missing a sporting event or class trip, write "game" or "trip" or draw a bus at Bus Stop 1.

CREATING A LAMENT

One positive way to deal with the hard things that happen in our lives is to create a lament, a way of expressing our pain to God. Lament can be done in words, music, dance, drawing, or any other form of creative expression.

A lament helps us expose all the stuff that we have tried to hide and share it with God instead. This is a good way to start telling your story, naming your feelings, and releasing painful memories. As it becomes more comfortable for you to share your pain privately with God, creating a lament can lead to sharing your story with another person when you are ready.

There are many examples of laments in the Bible. Trauma after trauma happened to the nation of Israel as a community (wars, captivity, displacement, famines) as well as to individuals (abuse, rape, abandonment, murder). Many people in the Bible found comfort in bringing their pain to God. They had an honest way of speaking to God where they poured out their complaints to him, sometimes even as they declared their trust in him.

A lament can have some or all of these different parts, but they all must have a complaint.

- Call out to God ("O God")
- Review of God's faithfulness in the past
- **Tell God your complaints and pain**
- Ask God for help
- Affirm your trust in God

Take some time to create a lament. Read **PSALM 13** if you need help, or think of what questions you would like to ask God about the difficult things in your life. You can put your lament in writing, song, rap, poem, prayer, or any creative way you wish to express your inner feelings to God. It does not have to include all five parts of a lament listed above. When you

PSALM 13 (CEV)

How much longer, LORD,
  will you forget about me?
Will it be forever?
  How long will you hide?
How long must I be confused
  and miserable all day?
How long will my enemies
  keep beating me down?

Please listen, LORD God,
  and answer my prayers.
Make my eyes sparkle again,
  or else I will fall
  into the sleep of death.
My enemies will say,
  "Now we've won!"
They will be greatly pleased
  when I am defeated.

I trust your love,
and I feel like celebrating
  because you rescued me.
You have been good to me, LORD,
  and I will sing about you.

have finished, consider sharing your lament with someone else who is going through circumstances similar to your own.

MY LAMENT

MY MANIFESTO

Sometimes living through hard times forces us to evaluate what we believe about God and decide what is really important in our lives. Have you ever had those thoughts?

A declaration of your beliefs and values is called a manifesto. When you take time to think about what's really important to you and what you believe in, it can help you align your life goals with those things, and you will feel more confident and empowered to move forward with hope.

Finish the sentences on the next page to get you started, then add your own if you'd like. Don't forget to sign it!

This is personal to you. But a manifesto is often a public declaration, so consider sharing what you have written with someone else. It may encourage others to think about these things, as well. You may want to take a picture of it and make it your phone background to remind yourself of your manifesto.

MY MANIFESTO

IT IS IMPORTANT TO ME that people _______________________________________

____

I AM
PASSIONATE
ABOUT

MY HEART BREAKS when

I'm surprised by ____

I want others to see me as ____

FEARS & FAILURES that have shaped me

I BELIEVE GOD CAN

What gives my life
MEANING & PURPOSE

Things that
GIVE ME PEACE

I VALUE

I BELIEVE

SIGNATURE

PEACE, BE STILL

You have been living in some difficult circumstances. Let's find out what Jesus did in a crazy situation when everyone around him was worried and afraid.

Before this incident happened, Jesus had been sitting in a boat all day long, teaching a huge crowd of people on the shore, and he was exhausted. We pick up the story from there, found in the Bible in the Gospel according to Mark (**MARK 4:36–41**).

> And leaving the crowd behind, they took him with them in the boat, just as he was. And other boats were with him. A great windstorm arose, and the waves were breaking into the boat, so that the boat was already filling with water. But he was in the stern, asleep on the cushion. All of the people in the boats were afraid that their boats would be broken into pieces and they would all drown. They woke him and said to him, "Teacher, do you not care that we are perishing?" And he awoke and rebuked the wind and said to the sea, "Peace! Be still!" And the wind ceased, and there was a great calm. He said to them, "Why are you so afraid? Have you still no faith?" And they were filled with great fear and said to one another, "Who then is this, that even the wind and the sea obey him?"

These crazy days are like a terrible storm in our lives. Many people feel stuck because everything about the future is unknown. One of the ways to feel less stuck is to ask Jesus to calm our fears and worries that are like the wind and the waves.

TALK ABOUT IT

1. Why did his friends think Jesus didn't care about them?

2. When he said, "Peace! Be still!" why did the wind and the sea obey him? (Check out **COLOSSIANS 1:16–17** in the Bible.)

3. Why were his friends afraid when the wind stopped blowing and the waves became calm? (Do you think it was because Jesus was even more powerful than the storm?)

4. What is the biggest storm in your life right now?

If Jesus were sitting next to you right now, he might be saying, "Peace, be still," or maybe these things:

"Be still and know that I am God." **PSALM 46:10**

"I will never leave you nor forsake you." **HEBREWS 13:5b**

"Don't be afraid . . . Take courage! I am here!" **MARK 6:50b**

**Jesus can give you a sense of peace
that you will not find anywhere else.
All you need to do is ask him.**

If you would like to find out more about knowing God, your pastor, priest, or other church leader would be happy to talk with you.

Getting Help

This book has many things that you can do by yourself to feel better and start to move forward with life. Hopefully, some of the stories or activities have been helpful for you. However, they may not be enough. One thing we saw in the story was how helpful it was for Rosa and Phoenix to find someone to talk to. They realized that they could talk to each other and that there were good, safe adults to talk to, as well.

You may need someone to talk to, too. Think of who that may be. Telling your story releases the power it can have over you.

Sometimes difficult feelings can be so overwhelming that people might hurt themselves. If you ever feel like hurting yourself in any way, talk to someone that you feel safe with.

In the Bible, **DEUTERONOMY 31:6** says, **"Be strong and courageous. Do not be afraid or terrified because of them, for the LORD your God goes with you; he will never leave you nor forsake you."**

DON'T FORGET—YOU'RE NOT ALONE. GOD IS WITH YOU. HE SEES YOU AND HE HEARS YOU.

More Resources

VIDEOS

Use the QR code to see this playlist online for videos illustrating the **Hiding Our Feelings** activity (page 41) and **How Our Brains React to Danger** (page 42).

BEYOND DISASTER

UNSTUCK is part of the **Beyond Disaster** series. At the website **BeyondDisaster.Bible**, you will also find resources for adults *(Beyond Disaster: A Survivor's Guide for Spiritual First Aid)* and children *(God Is With Me: A Family Guide to Living After Disaster)* in several languages.

TRAUMA HEALING BASICS

For more resources on understanding trauma and supporting mental health with the time-tested wisdom of the Bible, visit **TraumaHealingBasics.org**.

WHAT DID YOU THINK?

We would love to hear about your experience with *UNSTUCK*.

- **Participants!** Please use the blue QR code here to give us a quick rating and comment.

- **Leaders!** If you're **not** a trauma healing facilitator, please use the black QR code to the right to tell us about your groups and your thoughts.

- **Facilitators!** If you're signed up as a trauma healing facilitator, please submit a report on each of your gatherings in the facilitator area on **traumahealinginstitute.org**.

Journal

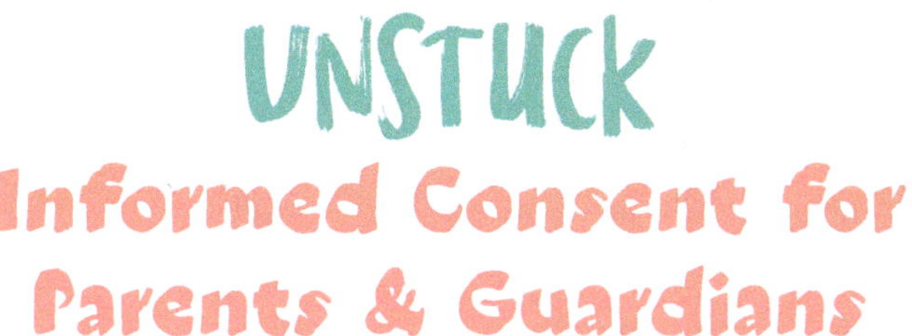

UNSTUCK: A Guide for Living in Uncertain Times is a Bible-based interactive booklet to help young people cope with grief and anxiety caused by difficult circumstances following a disaster. Youth will learn to recognize their losses, tell their stories, connect with feelings, and find strategies for moving forward in the midst of a crisis.

A small group using UNSTUCK will provide participants an opportunity to connect meaningfully with others their age under the guidance of experienced youth ministry workers. The small group experience will be a safe place for them to find healing from some of the hurts they have had as a result of this crisis.

The group will include five sessions addressing questions that youth may be struggling with.

1. Why am I feeling this way?
2. What can I do with my feelings?
3. How do I get unstuck?
4. What is happening inside me?
5. How can I relate to God in uncertain times?

Due to the sensitive nature of this work, we practice confidentiality to create a safe place for participants to openly and honestly share. However, the law mandates that we report concerns for the safety and wellbeing of the minors we serve. Therefore, we will notify appropriate parties if teens share an intent to hurt self or others, or if there are concerns of child abuse or neglect.

Parents/Legal Guardians: Please sign the permission statement below if you support your teen's decision to participate in this group, and return it to the group leaders.

I give my permission for ______________________________________ to participate in this group. I understand that I can seek further information by contacting the group leaders.

____

Parent/Legal Guardian (please print)   *Signature*   *Today's Date*

Location: ❑ Online   ❑ In Person ________________________________

Dates: ____

Group Leaders:

Name	Organization	Email

www.ingramcontent.com/pod-product-compliance
Lightning Source LLC
Chambersburg PA
CBHW080756030726
47593CB00007B/2396